BBC MUSIC GUIDES

———

DEBUSSY ORCHESTRAL MUSIC

BBC MUSIC GUIDES

Debussy Orchestral Music

DAVID COX

UNIVERSITY OF WASHINGTON PRESS
SEATTLE

List of works discussed

First published 1974 by the British Broadcasting Corporation
Copyright © David Cox 1974
University of Washington Press edition first published 1975
Library of Congress Catalog Card Number 74-19974
ISBN 0-295-95374-8
Printed in England

Introduction

The full impact of the new musical landscape which Debussy created comes across to us most clearly, most explicitly, in his orchestral works. It is the impact of an imagination sensual and picturesque, deriving its energy and meaning from an acutely sensitive response to the world of nature and the symbolism of the arts in general.

Debussy fiercely defended his independence. 'I make music in order to serve my art to the best of my ability and without any other preoccupation.' He worked hard, never satisfied, but (from his student days) always knowing the direction in which he wanted to go. He cared little about the controversies which his works so often provoked, and was largely indifferent to the praise or disapproval of the critics and the public. Disliking publicity and *arrivisme,* he preferred a withdrawn kind of life, away from the tumult but extremely sensitive to all that was going on around him, needing and enjoying carefully chosen friendships, seeking freedom of expression in his life as in his art – hating systems and rules. *'Il faut n'écouter les conseils de personne, mais du vent qui passe et nous raconte l'histoire du monde.'* ('We must not listen to the advice of anyone, except of the fleeting wind which tells us the history of the world.') He wanted to do and express only what he really felt, cultivating the passing moment, the life of the senses: music as immediate reality.

In the early years of this century Debussy once wrote: 'Every sound we hear around us can be reproduced. Everything that a keen ear perceives in the rhythm of the surrounding world can be represented musically.' This is very similar to something Vaughan Williams said at about the same time: 'Have we not all about us forms of musical expression which we can take and purify and raise to the level of great art?' The result in Debussy's case was a richly imaginative world of subtle harmonies and rhythms; melodies and chords drawn from the whole-tone and other unusual scales; chords regarded as colour, and colour often as an end in itself; oriental flavour and design in ornamental passages; abrupt unprepared modulations, false relations, and rapidly-shifting tonal focal-points. As the poet Verlaine had suggested that the *poetic* image should be *plus vague et plus soluble dans l'air* – so too with music, more indefinite and more fluid in the air, with nothing to weigh it down.

Through this kind of freedom Debussy loosened classical tonality as such, but he did not destroy it, as Schoenberg felt obliged to do. Focal points remained, however flexible. A richer, freer and essentially positive attitude towards tonality was the result of Debussy's experiences. He created a new, instinctive, dreamlike world of music, lyrical and pantheistic, contemplative and objective – a kind of art, in fact, which seemed to reach out into all aspects of experience. He admired Wagner's attempt to combine all the arts, and he was profoundly influenced harmonically by Wagner, but he hated the heroic style. Another very powerful influence was Russian: besides showing an interest in modal Russian folk music, Debussy also had the greatest admiration for the work of Mussorgsky, some of whose methods forestalled his own. He wrote: 'No one has given utterance to the best within us in terms more gentle and profound . . . Mussorgsky's art is spontaneous and free from arid formulas . . . The form of his music is so varied that by no possibility whatever can it be related to any established, one might say *official*, form, since it depends on and is made up of successive minute touches mysteriously linked together by means of an instinctive clairvoyance.'

In these words we might be reading a description of Debussy's own music – the *Prélude à l'Après-midi d'un Faune,* for example. Perhaps it is not surprising to find him writing about Mussorgsky in this way: in the Russian composer's *Pictures from an Exhibition,* originally for piano, each movement has a descriptive title (like Debussy's *Préludes*) but is always musically complete in itself; and although dating from as early as 1874, many passages are already very Debussy-ish – such as the combination of pentatonic melody, rhythmic flexibility, and harmonic richness in Ex. 1.

In the evolution of nineteenth- and twentieth-century music the piano has played a tremendously important role, and this is vitally relevant in considering any aspect of Debussy's art. Apart from the development of piano music as such, composers have found the piano a convenient and practical medium through which they can experiment with, and try out, whatever kind of music they are writing – be it orchestral, operatic, songs or chamber music. Most composers compose 'at the piano'. Stravinsky, in his autobiographical *Chroniques de ma Vie,* said: 'I think it is a thousand times preferable to compose in direct contact with the material of sound

Ex.1 (moderato)

[*la matière sonore*] than to compose by imagining that material.' This is the general rule, but there are probably many exceptions. (For example, Berlioz, who was not a pianist, could throw himself directly into the sea of orchestral sounds, and surely he must have written his works straight into full score.) The piano is a suggestive instrument, a medium of imitation and associations. Somehow an instrument which is basically percussive – the action of hammers on stretched strings – can become, in sensitive hands, an expressive, singing medium. And of course this is achieved only by an elaborate deception in which the imagination of both composer and listener is involved. It is in fact the message taking over the medium. At least on the piano every note of a piece of music can be played with a different feeling and a different intensity – light and shade are fully controlled. When there is extreme musical sensitivity and imagination (as with Debussy) we can be unaware that any element is lacking in the piano medium – even the basic inability to sustain the tone.

Such was the instrument through which Debussy constantly worked; and his principal model was Chopin. The impression of the piano-playing of Debussy, for those who were fortunate enough to hear it in the flesh, must have been in many ways similar to Chopin's. 'You must forget that the piano has hammers' was one of his sayings. The pianist Marguerite Long, who worked extensively with him, described Debussy as an incomparable pianist. In her book *Au piano avec Debussy*, she wrote: 'How can I ever forget the suppleness, the caress, the depth of his touch? While his fingers seemed to glide over the keyboard with a lightness and at the same

7

time a penetration, by subtle pressures he obtained a tone of extra-ordinary expressive range.' What is important is that the piano became in every way a natural part of him (as it was with Chopin) – a living and sensitive extension through which every shade of the musical personality could find complete expression, at the same time exploring all the possibilities of timbre and contrast available.

Marguerite Long has also told us of Debussy's admiration for Bach, Mozart and Chopin – and especially Chopin, she said, on the subject of whom he was inexhaustible. From his student days, he was *impregnated* with Chopin; Chopin almost seemed to be dwelling within him; and he sought in his own performances what he thought to be the very procedures of the Polish master. We have indeed a very close parallel between Chopin and Debussy. With Chopin, the originality of the compositions was at one with the highly individual style of piano-playing: by means of touch, personality, the most ingenious technical manipulation, the development of the finest detail – in fact by extreme art – he stimulated the listener's imagination in ways that were new and adventurous, extending by experiment, or by logical musical compulsion, or by the very placing of the fingers themselves, the accepted harmonic range of his time.

So it was with Debussy. The new world which he was discovering was, in essence, most conveniently explored by means of the piano. Yet in the final expression of important musical ideas it was only comparatively late in his career that Debussy was prepared to trust to the suggestiveness of the piano as a solo medium. Before that, he preferred the explicit colours of the orchestra. The degree to which piano and orchestra could be subtly one and the same for him as a personal means of expression is shown by Gustave Doret's description of the composer's 'perfect performance' of the *Prélude à l'Après-midi d'un Faune* (see p. 12).

In the early years of this century, at about the same time that Schoenberg, in *Das Buch der hängenden Gärten,* achieved in his way the liquidation of tonality, we find Debussy writing to a friend as follows: 'I am more and more convinced that music is not a thing which can be cast naturally into a traditional and fixed form. It is made up of tone-colours and rhythms. The rest is a lot of humbug invented by frigid imbeciles riding on the backs of the Masters. . . . Music is a young art from the point of view of technique as well as knowledge.'

The new freedom for Debussy came through a world of suggestion and symbol, closely related to the poetry and visual arts of
his day, with which he was intimately associated. A comparison
with Impressionism in painting is possible, but can be misleading.
The Impressionist painters set about representing exactly what the
eye sees. This sometimes led to unfocused outlines, casual composition and vivid colours. A painter such as Monet might be
concerned with light *as* light in a way arguably similar to Debussy's
sentiate use of sound *as* sound. But a more meaningful comparison is
with Symbolism, in both painting and poetry, which was in complete
contrast to Impressionism: it *suggested* ideas and states of mind by
means of symbols which became *more* significant, in the inner world
of reflection, than any external reality. In this the inspiration may
have been certain kinds of oriental art (including Japanese) which
were in vogue at the time in Paris. (At one stage Debussy was
certainly influenced by Javanese music.) Cézanne said that in his
painting he had not tried to reproduce nature, but to represent it.
Similarly, among the Symbolist poets, Mallarmé held that to name
an object was to destroy it; but to suggest it – that was his dream.
Debussy, a great friend of Mallarmé, found his first really characteristic expression with his orchestral piece conveying the emotion
and significance of the Mallarmé poem *L'Après-midi d'un Faune*.
Many of Debussy's most satisfying songs are settings of Symbolist
poems – of Verlaine and Baudelaire. It was as though he recognised
in Verlaine something of a kindred spirit, sensitive, highly sensual,
ruthless; someone who could distil from suffering and unrest the
most penetrating poetry – as he himself could distil the most
penetrating music. Symbolism in painting prepared the way for
every form of contemporary visual art: and Debussy's important
compositions had equally far-reaching effects on the music of the
twentieth century.

Prélude à l'Après-midi d'un Faune

O nymphes, regonflons des SOUVENIRS divers.
'Mon œil, trouant les joncs, dardait chaque encolure
Immortelle, qui noie en l'onde sa brûlure
Avec un cri de rage au ciel de la forêt;

9

Et le splendide bain de cheveux disparaît
Dans les clartés et les frissons, ô pierreries! . . .'
(O nymphs, let us bring back to life those many different memories.
My eye, piercing the reeds, fixed on each immortal figure as it
slaked its burning in the cooling waters, crying in frustration to the
forest sky; and the splendour of hair disappears in the shuddering
and jewelled brightness.)

Stéphane Mallarmé's 116-line poem *L'Après-midi d'un Faune* – of
which the above is an excerpt – was one aspect of an important
intermingling of the arts which took place under that title.
Mallarmé himself testified that such a poem (with its suggestions,
its symbolism, its sounds often used for their own sake) is itself
inspired by music – or perhaps (in a well-known phrase) aspiring
to the state of music. Debussy described his *Prélude* as 'a general
impression of the poem', but he was quite clear that it was not
programme music. 'It does not set out to be a synthesis of the
poem', he stated, 'it is rather a series of scenes against which the
desires and dreams of the faun are seen to stir in the afternoon
heat.' Later, the poem and music combined to give rise to one of
the most controversial of the Diaghilev ballets – with choreography by Nijinsky which was perhaps too crudely representational
an interpretation.

The origin of the poem goes back to a play, *Diane au bois* by
Théodore de Banville, which was produced in Paris in 1863. The
style and ideas of the play had an important influence on the 23-
year-old Mallarmé when, two years later, he wrote the first version
of the poem – then called *Monologue d'un Faune*. At first he had no
success with it, nor with a revised version. He had originally hoped
it would be performed on the stage by the actor Constant Coquelin;
but the poem was dismissed as untheatrical and lacking in clarity.
It was not till 1876 that Mallarmé published a final version – a
slim, elegant volume, with an illustration by Edouard Monet, and
with the title *L'Après-midi d'un Faune*. It was cited in J. K. Huysmans' most famous novel *À rebours* ('Against the Grain') which
appeared in 1882. Debussy was then twenty and may well have
first heard of the poem through the Huysmans novel. It was
about this time that Debussy started work on an opera, based
(significantly enough) on Banville's play *Diane au bois,* mentioned
above. This project was abandoned. But two years later he made a
setting for voice and piano of Mallarmé's poem *Apparition*.

The personal friendship with Mallarmé began, it seems, through the informal seminars on poetry and the arts which the poet held at his apartments on Tuesday evenings. The poet's disciples included such names as Paul Claudel (who later collaborated with Honegger and Milhaud), Marcel Proust, André Gide. Debussy probably gained entrée to the Tuesday-evening meetings through the writer Pierre Louÿs, a very close friend of the composer ('of all my friends the one I have loved best', he once wrote). Mallarmé was the most musically-minded of poets, attending concerts regularly and even contributing an essay, 'Richard Wagner – rêverie d'un poète français', to the *Revue Wagnérienne*. Most poets tend to regard their own work as something complete in itself: Mallarmé seemed constantly to envy music its ability to free itself completely from everyday verbal and pictorial images and to convey 'the naked flesh of emotion'.

Mallarmé was still hoping for a theatrical presentation of *L'Après-midi d'un Faune*, and no doubt poet and composer discussed this in detail. Up to at least the spring of 1894, Debussy's forthcoming work was being described as *Prélude, Interludes, et Paraphrase finale* for Mallarmé's *L'Après-midi d'un Faune,* indicating incidental music for a stage production. We do not know precisely why the original idea was modified. Perhaps Debussy shared the view of the Comédie Française that Mallarmé's poem was non-theatrical. Perhaps he composed more music than was finally used in the *Prélude:* or the *Prélude* may be the quintessence of something larger – as indeed its quality suggests. We have Debussy's own account of Mallarmé's reactions to the completed *Prélude* after the composer had played it over to him, on the piano, at his flat in the Rue de Londres. In a letter to G. Jean-Aubry, written sixteen years later, Debussy wrote: 'Mallarmé came in with his prophetic air and wearing his Scottish plaid. After hearing it, he was silent for some time, and then said: "I never expected anything like that. The music draws out the emotion of my poem and gives it a warmer background than colour".' On a copy of *L'Après-midi d'un Faune* which Mallarmé sent Debussy after the first performance of the *Prélude*, the poet had written:

> Sylvain d'haleine première,
> Si ta flûte a réussi,
> Ouïs toute la lumière
> Qu'y soufflera Debussy.

(Spirit of the forest, if with your primal breath your flute sounds well, listen now to the radiance which comes when Debussy plays.) Mallarmé also said that the music explores much further the nostalgia of the poem – the evocation of a lost, instinctive and legendary world – and 'illumines it with subtlety, malaise, and richness'. The poem as a whole is a wealth of images and fertile imagination, but indefinite, artificial and mannered. Debussy's musical impression, by comparison, makes a direct appeal – the emotion is clearer – though the style is equally rich in colour and imagery.

The first performance was conducted by Gustave Doret. The Swiss composer and conductor was then twenty-eight years old and had been put in charge of a series of concerts given in Paris by the Société Nationale. In his memoirs Doret tells how Debussy took him to his apartment on the Rue Gustave Doré (a remarkable coincidence of names!), arranged the proofs of the orchestral score on the piano, and played the work through several times. Doret was completely captivated; he described his reactions to Debussy's playing: 'By what extraordinary gifts was he able to reproduce at the keyboard the colours of his orchestra, with the most perfect balance, even to the instrumental nuances? In its subtlety and profound sensibility it seemed to be the perfect interpretation.' They went on to discuss the great difficulties in preparing a satisfactory performance of the work, because of its new technique of orchestration.

Debussy, in his critical writings, was often outspoken about other composers' orchestration. Wagner, he said, relied on 'a species of polychromatic putty, spread almost uniformly', and it was no longer possible in his works to distinguish the sound of the violin from that of the trombone. On the other hand, he found the orchestration of *Parsifal*, in its way, 'infallible'. Again, writing under his pseudonym of 'Monsieur Croche', and not without a certain deliberate overstatement, he described Beethoven's orchestration as 'a formula of black and white, resulting in the whole exquisite gamut of greys'. Completely different from Elgar, who was constantly mixing his orchestral colours, Debussy himself aimed at a transparency of texture in which the different timbres do not lose their individuality. In particular he seemed to be attracted to the woodwind instruments, and wrote in a highly individual and extremely telling way for each of them. The potential of the harp also is fully realised. There are no vulgar realistic effects in his works, such as sometimes occur in Richard Strauss (bleating sheep, the baby crying in the bath, etc.). When the faun's pipe, or the sea, or the colours and rhythms of Spain are suggested by Debussy through texture and timbre, it is always with imagination and in ways that are satisfying in purely musical terms.

After much careful preparation, the *Prélude à l'Après-midi d'un Faune* was first performed on 22 December 1894 in the Salle d'Harcourt, Paris, at one of the concerts of the Société Nationale. The programme included works by Glazunov, Saint-Saëns, César Franck, and others less known. It is pleasant to note that the large audience responded enthusiastically to Debussy's very new-sounding piece. Conductor and composer were both satisfied with the performance. The importance of the work, however, was not appreciated at first, and critical reaction was generally unfavourable. A number of other performances followed. But it was only after the opera *Pelléas et Mélisande* had made Debussy world-famous and controversial that performances of *L'Après-midi* were given in other countries during the early years of this century – in the USA, Germany, Italy, Austria. Henry Wood introduced it to London in 1904. And in 1908 Debussy himself conducted it (and *La Mer*) in London at Queen's Hall. On this occasion the music critic of *The Times* wrote a dismal review of the concert. Today it is one of the most frequently performed of all French orchestral works, and is regarded not only as a landmark in the evolution of music, but also as one of the most evocative and enjoyable examples of Debussy's art.

The scoring of the *Prélude à l'Après-midi d'un Faune* is for three flutes, two oboes, cor anglais, two clarinets, two bassoons, four horns, two harps and the usual strings. In the last seventeen bars of the work, small antique cymbals are required – tiny metal plates of definite pitch – tuned to two notes. The dedication is to Raymond Bonheur, who had been a fellow-student at the Paris Conservatoire, and for a short time a close friend of Debussy.

(To print the title as *Prélude à l'après-midi d'un faune,* as is frequently done in France and other countries, is misleading and smacks of illiteracy. On the other hand, to put in quotation marks Mallarmé's title-within-the-title, *L'Après-midi d'un Faune,* would be very cumbersome, although strictly correct. Probably the compromise of *Prélude à l'Après-midi d'un Faune* is the most satisfactory.)

Why did this short musical work sound so new in 1894? And why does it still today retain its fresh, radiant quality? Consider first Debussy's own statements. In classical music the development, as it seemed to him, consisted of repetitions of the same *motifs*, the same themes. Can the same emotion be expressed twice? 'I shall achieve a music', he said, 'truly freed from *motifs*, or constructed on only one continuing *motif* which nothing interrupts, and which never goes back on itself. Then there will be logical development, very closely reasoned. There will *not* be, between two repetitions of the same *motif*, characteristic and commonplace filling-in, which is normally hasty and superfluous. The development will no longer be this mere amplification of material, but we shall come to regard it in a more universal light, and eventually in a more real and physical way.'

In artistic creation the thoughts, the ideas, and the style in which they find expression – all this is one process. Debussy's sensibility, the subtlety of his musical thought, impelled him towards extending the musical language – giving greater scope and flexibility to the forms in which the ideas eventually clothed themselves. The nearest ancestor is the symphonic poem – the musical form in which drama, emotion, scene-painting, story-telling are conveyed in purely instrumental terms. This form took shape in the mid-nineteenth century. An important factor in its development was Wagner's method of denoting a character by a theme (*Leitmotiv*) and changes in that character by the varying of the theme – as also was Liszt's romantic imagination, stimulated by literary and pictorial elements (in ways similar to Debussy's) which he translated into musical terms.

With Debussy, unity is achieved, but not by development or by form in the accepted sense – rather by 'successive minute touches mysteriously linked together by means of an instinctive clairvoyance' (as Debussy had perceived in Mussorgsky) – an equilibrium of feelings and textures, fluid, transparent, scattered in multiple nuances, the most delicate blending of light and shade.

The opening theme, on the flute,

Ex. 2

Très modéré

p doux et expressif

is the principal *motif*, the main generating symbol of the work. Each time the idea recurs it is in a different transformation: nothing is repeated in the same form. Harmonic adventurousness is suggested from the start by the interval of an augmented fourth, between which the unaccompanied flute rises and falls in the first two bars. Debussy did not show 'reverence for the key' (as he called it), but sought through an attenuated tonality '*a mode that tries to contain all the nuances*', including harmonic progressions with a subtle logic of their own. The subtlety of rhythm also, in the opening phrase, is consistent with the flexibility which is a feature of the work as a whole. The arabesque-like writing – influenced probably by the orientalisms which Debussy would have found in Borodin, Rimsky-Korsakov and other Russian composers – has an improvisatory quality, a mosaic structure, which nevertheless is unified.

The opening thirty bars consist basically of four presentations of the principal theme, each with different harmony and treatment, and differently extended. The first contains a sudden complete bar of silence and expectation (bar 6), remarkable in the context. The second builds up to a rich and full orchestral sound; and the third and fourth present rhythmic variations, leading to a full close in B major, the only definite cadence and point of repose in the whole work until the last page.

So far, this very roughly corresponds to an 'exposition' section. Now begins a kind of 'development' during the next twenty-four bars. The first bars of this part (Ex. 3 overleaf) are of particular interest in that the textures of sound, besides being novel in effect, look forward to the 'fragmented' methods of *Jeux* some twenty years later, and also to the style which Stravinsky was to develop, under the strong influence of Debussy. This use of instrumental colour as an end in itself – in a way similar to the *pointilliste* technique in painting – was something new: after the *sforzando* chord by the muted horns, the harp picks out and underlines the note B in octaves, the second violins and violas have one isolated chord mixing with the horns, the cellos rapidly reiterate a C♯, and so on. Also, the whole-tone scale is used, in melody and harmony, in the last two bars – growing naturally, one feels, from the tritone interval of the principal theme (Ex. 2), but used only as a passing effect (nowhere else in the work is the whole-tone aspect isolated in this way). A lyrical,

Ex. 3

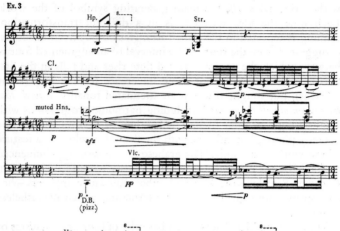

expansive section, which gradually animates and reaches a moderate climax, begins with a theme on the oboe, *doux et expressif*, closely related in shape to the opening:

Ex. 4

The figures marked *a* and *b* are used for development and modulation, and *b* – the syncopated *motif* – is also used for a four-bar

clarinet episode over a pedal-note, A♭, which becomes the dominant of D♭ major, the key of the work's 'middle section' that follows. This warmly sustained interlude is based on a theme reminiscent of the D flat Nocturne (Op. 27, no. 2) of Chopin, who, as already noted, was one of the main influences in Debussy's development.

Ex. 5

The figure marked *b* in Ex. 4, and its extension, is combined with this theme in five cadential bars. Next, in E major, we have a development of the principal flute theme, in augmentation – a version without tritone, which has now become directly reminiscent of a phrase in the famous duet 'Mon coeur s'ouvre à ta voix' from Saint-Saëns's opera *Samson et Délilah* (the phrase in question is to the words 'Ah, réponds à ma tendresse'), which similarly uses flute, harp arpeggios and long-held string chords. We know that Debussy admired Saint-Saëns's opera when it was produced in Paris in 1890 (but admiration was not mutual – Saint-Saëns consistently disliked Debussy and his music). The two augmented statements of the principal theme are interrupted by brief and delicate scherzo-like episodes, the second of which leads back to the mood and tempo of the opening section of the work, but 'avec plus de langueur': a kind of 'recapitulation', but in different clothing, with two more presentations of the main theme – the first (over a pedal note E) ambiguous in tonality and combining with Ex. 4, figure *b*; the second more clearly in C♯ major, and *without* tritone – a solo cello playing in octaves with the flute. Three bars of modulation lead to a chord with B in the bass, becoming the dominant of E major, and over a pedal note of E this is definitely established as the final key in the five coda-like bars. Muted horns combine with the first violins – a strange, haunting effect – in a final chordal memory of the flute theme. Debussy said that the close of the work represented a prolongation of the last line of the poem:

'Couple, adieu! Je vais voir l'ombre que tu devins.'

Flesh and spirit become a memory; the experience continues to reverberate inwardly.

It has been called the first Impressionist work in music. Impres-

sionism, originally a term of abuse in the visual arts, can be misleading, suggesting vagueness and dreamlike imprecision. In the
case of Debussy's music this is very wide of the mark. A study of
the score of *L'Après-midi* reveals complete clarity of thought,
precision over details, and (as the above outline shows) a definite
sense of form, not unlike rondo in character, but always with a
remarkable variety of content and texture, extremely sensitive in
every way to the immediate effect, enjoying a freedom of invention
which is never without purpose. Every note, every dynamic mark
tells; nothing is superfluous. The tone-colour and capabilities of
each of the different instruments are explored with unerring instinct and secure knowledge. The use of the harps is integral –
never mere decoration. The writing for the horns is particularly
imaginative, ranging from full-bodied support and prominent
melodic statement to delicate interweaving, blending and sustain-
ing, and with carefully-judged use of occasional muted effects.
There is also a wide range of colour in the string-writing, including
soft tremolando chords played near the middle of the strings
(*sul tasto*), delicate staccato chords (*avec sourdine* – muted), and
division into eight parts. The small antique tuned cymbals are
reserved for the last section, tuned to E and B, the tonic and
dominant of the 'home' key. They emphasise the ritual nature of
the work. (Stravinsky was later to use them, also with ritualistic
effect, but in a far more emphatic treatment, at the conclusion of
Les Noces.)

As for the solo flute – it came into its own and found its true
personality as never before. From its opening notes it breathed a
new life into the art of music.

Nocturnes

The *Prélude à l'Après-midi d'un Faune* is a superb example of the
translation of sensual and emotional impressions into the symbolic
language of music. The process was continued in Debussy's next
important orchestral work, the three *Nocturnes*.

The original conception of this work was very different from the
form in which we now know it. Towards the end of 1894 – the
year in which an entire concert of Debussy's works was given in
Brussels – Debussy wrote to the Belgian violinist Eugène Ysaÿe:

'I am working on three Nocturnes for violin and orchestra that are intended for you. The first is scored for strings; the second for three flutes, four horns, three trumpets and two harps; the third is a combination of both these groups.' He goes on: 'This is, in fact, an experiment in the various arrangements that can be made with a single colour – like the study of grey in painting.'

The title could have been suggested by the series of paintings entitled 'Nocturnes' by Whistler, whom Debussy greatly admired. The composer explained further: 'The title *Nocturnes* is to be interpreted in a general and, more specifically, in a decorative sense. Therefore it is not meant to designate the usual form of the Nocturne, but rather all the various impressions and the special effects of light that the word suggests.'

For musicians the word primarily suggests a fairly short, romantic, expressive, decorated form for piano – not necessarily night-music in any sense – originated by the Irish composer John Field and developed by Chopin. Debussy, with his liking for arabesque style, may have had Chopin in mind when he originally planned this work, intending to explore in his own way a decorative type of writing, in terms not of the piano but the solo violin. Two years later, in 1896, Debussy wrote again to Ysaÿe saying that he would prefer to delay the first performance of the *Nocturnes* until Ysaÿe could give it in Brussels. Did a score then exist in a version for violin and orchestra? Nobody has seen it. All we know is that between 1897 and 1899 Debussy composed or rearranged the *Nocturnes* as we now know them, in full orchestral clothing, but without a solo instrument. The composer and conductor Camille Chevillard directed the first performance, in Paris, at one of the Concerts Lamoureux in 1900: this was of two movements only – *Nuages* and *Fêtes*. The complete work was not heard until the following year.

Edward Lockspeiser, in his biography of the composer,[1] has suggested that the origin of the *Nocturnes* is earlier than the work for violin and orchestra intended for Ysaÿe. He links it with the *Trois Scènes au Crépuscule* which is mentioned by Debussy in 1892 as 'almost finished – that is to say, the orchestration is entirely planned and it is just a matter of writing out a full score'. Lockspeiser believed this to be the first form in which the *Nocturnes* took shape. How far, if at all, they resembled the version which

[1] Edward Lockspeiser, *Debussy: his life and mind* (London, 1962 and 1965).

was finally published we do not know, because the score has disappeared (if there was one). We know no more about the music of that version than we do about the violin-and-orchestra version – if indeed there *is* a connection between them. We know, however, that the three *Scènes au Crépuscule* were apparently inspired by a series of poems (under the same title) by Henri de Régnier, and the imagery of one of these poems, associated with musical instruments, trumpets and flutes, could well have inspired *Fêtes*. (A later poem of Régnier called 'La Vigile des Grèves' is also relevant, with its references to 'a procession of flutes' and 'the brilliance of angry tambourines and sharp trumpet calls'.) We find also a reference to a female choir – a possible connection with *Sirènes*. Another reference to the origin of the *Nocturnes* is given by Léon Vallas in an account of a conversation between the composer and his friend Paul Poujaud: 'One day, in stormy weather, as Debussy was crossing the Pont de la Concorde in Paris with Poujaud, he told him that on a similar kind of day the idea of the symphonic work *Nuages* had occurred to him: he had visualised those very thunder-clouds swept along by a stormy wind; a boat passing, its hooter sounding. These two impressions are recalled in the languorous succession of chords and by the short chromatic theme on the cor anglais.'[1]

Elsewhere, in a 'programme' of the work, Debussy wrote that '*Nuages* renders the unchanging aspect of the sky and the slow, solemn motion of the clouds, fading away in grey tones lightly tinged with white'. Affected as he was by the visual arts, as well as by poetry, Debussy may have been influenced by Turner's landscapes and their characteristic effects of light and pure colour. For Debussy, Turner, the forerunner of so-called Impressionism in painting, was 'the greatest creator of mysterious effects in the whole world of art'. But he hated the label 'Impressionism' applied to his music. In the popular mind the word suggests something vague, imprecise, groping – the very opposite of Debussy's clear and carefully-judged textures. A truer definition of Impressionism would be a portrayal of reality by reproducing an immediate visual experience – a direct though not sharply-focused impression of colour and shape, definite in expression, but free of orthodox stylisation. Here we can certainly find a parallel between Impressionism and the music of Debussy.

[1] Quoted in Lockspeiser, *op. cit.*

Association of ideas may enhance the experience of a musical work, but in the end it is the music that matters, whether it be *Nuages gris* by Liszt, or Mendelssohn's *Fingal's Cave* Overture, or a so-called 'pictorial' work of Debussy. Musically, much has been made of the fact that the opening bars of *Nuages*, the first of the *Nocturnes*, resembles a phrase in Mussorgsky's *Sunless* song-cycle. Certainly the shape is the same, but the purpose and feeling in the Mussorgsky song is completely different, and it consists of thirds and sixths, not thirds and fifths as in Debussy, for whom the idea may well have sprung originally from the fingers wandering *rêveusement* on the keys of the piano, with possibly an unconscious memory of Mussorgsky (whom he held in such high esteem):

Ex. 6

The movement seems to grow naturally from this initial idea, with contrasts of texture between woodwind and strings (muted, and with much subdividing), and from it fragmentary melodic *motifs* emerge, notably the cor anglais phrase:

Ex. 7

There is a contrasting pentatonic theme:

Ex. 8

first on flute and harp, then on solo violin, viola and cello in double octaves, treated with the same floating quality as the initial musical idea. Finally, the early material becomes broken up, and the clouds disperse into thin air . . . In all, this movement is one of the most personal and characteristic expressions of the composer.

Fêtes, the second of the *Nocturnes*, is clear and straightforward in form and content. The sky is cloudless and all is joyful animation, colour and excitement. Debussy is said to have told his friend Poujaud that *Fêtes* had been inspired by a recollection of old-time merrymaking in the Bois de Boulogne, attended by happy thronging crowds, with a procession of the former drum-and-bugle band of the Garde Nationale beating the tattoo as it approached from afar and passed out of sight. It is likely also that Debussy had in mind the military processions in Paris at the time of the Franco-Russian alliance. But impressions of this sort are transformed as they pass through the extreme sensitivity of the composer. His own description is imaginative and symbolic: '*Fêtes* gives us the vibrating dancing rhythm of the atmosphere with sudden flashes of light. There is also the episode of the procession (a dazzling, fantastic vision) which makes its way through the festive scene and becomes merged in it. But the background remains persistently the same; the festival with its blending of music and luminous dust participating in the cosmic rhythm.'

The 'cosmic' rhythm is given out by the strings at the very beginning and is an important unifying ingredient of the piece:

Ex. 9

On this background the woodwind play the joyous extroverted theme from which the whole of the first section of the piece is constructed:

Ex. 10

The orchestra used in these three *Nocturnes* is basically eleven woodwind, four horns, two harps and strings. The timpani have one or two important quiet effects in *Nuages,* and a female choir is added as a prominent colour in *Sirènes*. For *Fêtes* three trumpets, three trombones, cymbals and side-drum, besides timpani, are included. Muted brass in *Fêtes* is used in new and striking ways; and again subdivided strings are a regular feature in the scoring. On a basis of exuberance, the score is precisely and minutely calculated, always completely clear in its effects, using thematic development in a more traditional way than in either *Nuages* or *Sirènes*. About halfway through there is a sudden lull in the festivities – a throbbing rhythm persists softly in the background, and a new musical idea is presented: from the distance the 'dazzling fantastic vision' of the procession gradually approaches and becomes convincingly blended and unified with the carnival music. The final section of *Fêtes* is a reprise of the opening music, in modified forms, building up again, and subsiding – at the end disintegrating, but maintaining musical and rhythmic precision and purpose.

Sirènes depicts 'the sea and its countless rhythms', the composer has written; 'and presently, amongst the waves, silvered by the moonlight, is heard the mysterious song of the Sirens as they laugh and pass on'. If the original inspiration was a literary one, it might have been Régnier's poem 'L'Homme et la Sirène' or Swinburne's 'Nocturne', both of which are concerned with mermaids and their effects on mortals. Musically, it is an example of Debussy's love of decoration, of arabesque, such as he used in *L'Après-midi*, and it becomes one of the most important elements in a composition. The music is completely without thematic development in the traditional sense. Tremolando chords in the strings, arpeggio figures in woodwind, shimmering harps, the voices of the sirens (8 sopranos, 8 mezzos) used instrumentally, wordlessly, as colour, hypnotically – everything is basically static, like the sea itself, with variety and subtlety of rhythm only on the surface. Fundamentally, the music revolves round the interval of a second (Ex. 11), appoggiatura-like and obsessive, first heard in the horns at the opening (a), and becoming only slightly extended melodically (b):

Ex. 11

Above and below the undulating figure, at different levels, there are changing colours, flexible and varying rhythms and harmony, which create a haunting image of extraordinary beauty and richness.

Debussy (as was his custom) revised the orchestration of *Images* quite considerably after its first publication. In 1930, twelve years after the composer's death, a definitive edition was published, incorporating the changes made by him over the years – changes written into his own copy of the score. The differences were mostly in *Fêtes* and *Sirènes*.

La Mer

There is no overall unity about the *Nocturnes* we have just been discussing, because each movement is quite different in style and texture from the others. The same is not true of *La Mer* – which is in fact the best symphony ever written by a Frenchman. It is described by the composer (on the score) as 'Three Symphonic Sketches' – but there is nothing sketchy about them. Though not constructed along traditional lines, each is a finished, beautifully-wrought, cogent symphonic movement, the middle one being a scherzo – and considered together they form a perfectly unified composition, fulfilling in fact the requirements of a symphony as generally understood: that is to say, the work as a whole is large in conception, wide in its powers of suggestion, the structural elements (melody, harmony, rhythm) all of equal importance throughout; the diverse elements are fused into an organic whole, and motifs which unify the entire work are heard in the first few bars. For such a work to be truly characteristic of a French composer is rare. Before discussing *La Mer* in greater detail, perhaps some explanation can be found as to why truly French symphonies which satisfy are hard to find.

When Saint-Saëns, the eighteen-year-old Bizet, d'Indy, Chausson, Gounod, Dukas and others wrote symphonies, they were writing under strong Teutonic influence, and arguably against the grain – against the natural characteristics of the French. It is, I think, true to say that *all* music which we find meaningful and satisfying, of whatever country, is written as a result of a subtle and often unconscious integration, involving certain racial characteristics and inspiration from the musical heritage of the composer's own country, which (in conjunction with other outside influences) results in a style and in ideas which are both personal and universal. The Austro-German symphony developed from *its* natural background, first as an attitude to tonality, through dramatic contrasts and gradually widening expressive range; later, as a vehicle for personal and romantic feeling, which reached its furthest extreme in Mahler, for whom the medium of the symphony could contain the whole of life, from its simplest to its most complex aspects – the total experience, from the ugly and trivial to the beautiful and lofty. After hearing the Third Symphony of Mahler, Schoenberg wrote to his fellow-composer as follows: 'I think I have experienced your symphony. I felt the pain of one disillusioned; I saw the forces of evil and good contending; I saw a man in a torment of emotion exerting himself to gain inner harmony. I sensed a human being, drama, *truth*, the most ruthless truth.'

That quotation seems to clarify the essential difference between German and French music. To a French composer such a conception would be quite antipathetic. Why? The Latin temperament is animated, voluble, demonstrative, often gay, often quick-tempered but nevertheless tolerant, and at the same time distrusting of human nature (a characteristic often mistaken for cynicism, but really a sort of tolerant realism). A striking definition of the average Frenchman was once given by General De Gaulle: 'This Frenchman, who takes so much pain to be orderly in his thinking and so little in his actions, this logician always torn by doubt, this careless hard worker, this imperial adventurer who loves nothing more than his hearth and home, this fervent admirer of alexandrine verses, tailcoats and royal gardens, who nevertheless sings popular songs, dresses carelessly and litters his own lawns . . . this uncertain, unstable and contradictory people.'

In music the Frenchman will be orderly and precise in the smaller forms, but will probably feel no need or wish to undergo the immense mental discipline required for a large, unified musical structure. His shrewd sense of realism will find excuse by calling it a dislike of pretentiousness. French music is characterised by formal conciseness, more episodic expression, clarity of thought and feeling, careful and precise craftsmanship. We can also find in French taste an uncomplicated love of pleasure and avoidance of pain – a voluptuous enjoyment of sound as sound, without any of the Germanic feeling of *guilt*, an enjoyment too of colour for its own sake. In the background is the spirit of Couperin and Rameau, with their sensibility, charm, deftness of touch, essential simplicity of utterance. The spirit is aristocratic, courtly, rather than 'of the people'; sophisticated, witty, appealing rather to an *élite* – music of the intelligence and the senses, rather than that of introspection and abstraction. For Debussy, the large-scale structures of another great French composer, Berlioz, were anathema. He described the *Symphonie Fantastique* as 'that feverish masterpiece of romantic ardour which leaves one amazed that the music can interpret such extravagant situations without losing breath'. Debussy found his own cogent and compelling forms of expression in which there was much convincing large-scale structure: the clearest demonstration of this was in *La Mer*.

Let us now look more closely at this orchestral masterpiece of Debussy – the most personal, wide-ranging and fully representative of his orchestral works. In the background is his close connection from childhood with the sea. The son of a sailor, he was constantly enthralled by stories of his father's journeys to far-off lands, and he cherished the idea of becoming a sailor himself. Temperamentally he would almost certainly have found the life unbearable; but the sea remained a passion and became a source of inspiration, involving memories, imagination, and the influence of other artistic works. He was deeply impressed by Turner's sea pictures, which he had probably seen exhibited in Paris and at London's National Gallery during his visits in 1902 and 1903, about the time when he was starting to compose *La Mer*. He would also have known Edgar Allan Poe's vivid descriptions of the sea in his writings. Another important influence was Japanese – the landscapes and seascapes of two artists in particular, Katsushika Hokusai and Ando Hiroshige, who became fashionable in Paris and had a strong influence on the art of the time. When the full score of *La Mer* was published, the cover design (at the composer's request) was a reproduction of the Hokusai print 'The Hollow of the Wave off Kanagawa' – wonderfully appropriate in its detailed stylisation, its decorative personal style and powerful atmosphere. Like Turner, Debussy had had personal experience of danger in storms at sea. We know that he was much affected by Turner's work generally, and it may well have been that artist's sea pictures which provided a strong initial stimulus for *La Mer*. When composing this work, Debussy spoke of 'endless memories' that were aroused – 'worth more than reality, which generally weighs down one's thoughts too heavily' – memories which had already provided an inspiration for *Sirènes* and the sea music of the opera *Pelléas et Mélisande*. After the self-imposed restrictions of style and expression in *Pelléas* (completed 1902) it was as though Debussy felt the immediate need, in *La Mer,* to swing over to a more robust, wide-spanning, outward-turning construction full of variety and rhythmic strength – and the result is a rich, evocative work of particular personal importance. There is no vagueness and imprecision in *La Mer*. The harmonic subtleties, the blending of colours, the atmosphere of each movement – everything is realised with the utmost clarity and technical assurance.

(1) *De l'aube à midi sur la mer*

The title which the composer originally thought of, for this first movement, was 'Mer belle aux Îles Sanguinaires' (the French name for Corsica and Sardinia). This is also the title of a short story by Camille Mauclair, apparently published in 1893. 'From dawn to midday at sea', as the composer eventually decided to call it, misleadingly suggests a precise 'programme' music. (Erik Satie, who also used elaborate titles, pulled Debussy's leg by saying that he liked it all, but especially the bit at a quarter to eleven.) Whatever extra-musical inspiration or associations there may be, the music of Debussy is always self-sufficient. But though form and content are here strong in themselves, we see them, as the composer did, against a many-sided background, a fusion of the arts, and a fusion of nature and art. The process is not a simple musical one.

In *La Mer* a full-sized symphony orchestra is used – including two harps and cor anglais as important tone-colour ingredients. Over a quiet drum-roll and pedal-note of B in the double-basses, the opening music symbolises pentatonically the sun rising in the East. Two important thematic ingredients appear which are used, cyclically, in the structure of both this and the last movement – Ex. 12 overleaf. The introduction leads directly into the first main section (*Modéré, sans lenteur*) where the oriental flavour becomes more definite: the rippling texture of the strings, the pentatonic wave-patterns in the woodwind (in consecutive fifths), the arpeggio figures in the harp parts, combine to make a gamelan-like sonority, against which the four horns present the principal theme, in octaves (Ex. 13).

The contrasting section is built on a striking figure in triple rhythm, suggestive of the heaving motion of the sea:

This idea, first presented by cellos (subdivided into four groups), is developed with great variety of texture to a climax, and subsides to a reminiscence of earlier material (part of Ex. 13), a sustained and quietly expressive passage for cor anglais and two solo cellos in unison. This leads to a solemn chordal passage for horns and bassoons, suggestive of awe and immensity (the idea is again developed at the end of the last movement), and the rhythmic figure of Ex. 12 (a) is again brought into prominence for the movement's emphatic conclusion.

(2) *Jeu de vagues* (Play of the waves)

The construction is far more complex than that of the outer movements. Taken as a whole it represents, in a kind of scherzo form, the rapidly-shifting play of light on the waters, which has suggested rapidly-shifting *musical* patterns – textures which change and overlap too quickly for development in the traditional sense and therefore become fragmented, decorative, moment-to-moment in a way that is new and prophetic. Add to that a use of timbre as an *essential* element in the construction. It is a mark of Debussy's extraordinary genius that he was able to unify, to bind together consistently, the extremely diverse textures and timbres, the ever-changing tonalities, which make up this movement. (The supreme example of this process is to be found later – in *Jeux*.) One way of enjoying this movement is simply to relax and allow the varied and delicate patterns of exhilarating sounds to produce their immediate effect. To indicate more precisely what is happening has its problems, but an overall impression of some sort can be attempted. With Debussy the *motif*, the pregnant phrase, is the generating force, and the ways in which structures are built are extremely personal and untraditional, usually defying formal analysis. The difficulty has been expressed by Pierre Boulez: 'A component section of a theme is defined as another is suggested; another phrase is added and we have the beginnings of a form. More material is added and we have a structure.'

The main thematic material can perhaps be summarised as shown in Ex. 15 overleaf. After some irregular chromatic patterns in the flutes and clarinets, a bar of rapidly-repeated trumpet notes leads to one of the principal motifs (a), played initially by cor anglais. The development of this idea is abruptly interrupted by three muted trumpets playing, *fortissimo,* a triplet chordal figure. Suddenly the surface of the water has changed. We have a gently animated passage for strings and woodwind, the thematic figure of which (b) will be important later. The harps have whole-tone *glissandi*; flutes and clarinets rapidly reiterate a chord which accompanies another im-

Ex. 15

portant thematic figure on the cor anglais (c). A form of the first four notes shortly afterwards becomes an *ostinato* figure in demisemiquavers (d) passed between woodwind and strings, and the construction is now very free and decorative. The textures, the scoring – everything is of the utmost delicacy. The rhythm and melody of the solo violin (e and f) crystallise some essential ingredients in the music's structure. The oboe recalls the first principal theme (a), shortly followed by the cellos' expressive return to the second of the cor anglais *motifs* (c) – meanwhile woodwind and brass explore and interchange the rhythmic pattern of (e). These ingredients are all developed in very free, decorative style. Following that, there begins a new version of material heard near the beginning of the movement (b). In conjunction with the new expressive phrase (g) there is now quite a lengthy 'development' section which proceeds (rather unexpectedly) in traditional style – development by imitation, all of it over an unmoving pedal-note (G♯), suggesting the unchanging depth and stillness beneath the moving surface. Only at the highest point of the climax does the pedal-note change, and at once the movement subsides to a quietly percussive murmuring, over which various solo wind instruments (including muted trumpet) sum up with a fragment of the first motto-theme of the movement (a), recollected in tranquillity.

(3) *Dialogue du vent et de la mer* (Dialogue of the wind and the sea) Over the upward-thrusting waves in tumult, the wind (represented by sustained woodwind and muted horns) blows downwards. Such is the first obvious image which is translated into musical language meaningful in itself. A good deal of the thematic material in this movement is taken directly from the first movement – which gives a rounded feeling to the work as a whole. After the *Jeu de vagues,* the structure appears comparatively straightforward. Muted trumpets (*forte, expressif*) reintroduce a motif from near the beginning of the work (Ex. 12b), and constructive use is also made of the earlier rhythmic two-note figure (Ex. 12a). Tension increases dramatically, leading to a theme (very characteristic of the composer) representing the wind – sustained, flexible – first played by oboes, cor anglais and first bassoon, against a choppy wave-pattern below, in the lower strings.

Ex. 16

Later this theme is developed extensively, and the fifth bar takes on a dance-like rhythm which is varied and becomes an independent entity in the music's growth. We hear another treatment of the solemn chordal section from the first movement, and this is used in the summing-up and coda, where feelings of awe and joyous acceptance are combined, and where the rhythms and melodic figures suggested by the sea are united in a single image. This final clarification is firmly in the key of D-flat major, but the characteristic sharpened fourth of the scale is included.

La Mer was completed in 1905: 'Sunday, 5th March at six o'clock in the evening', the composer added to the manuscript score. Seven months later, on 15 October, the first performance was given in Paris, at the Concerts Lamoureux, conducted by Camille Chevillard. The work caused much violent controversy. To one critic it conveyed grandeur and delicacy, it was the composer's finest work; to another everything was 'as lifeless as dried plants in a herbarium'. In one of his conversation-volumes, Stravinsky recalled that Debussy once talked to him about the first performance of La Mer: 'The violinists flagged the tips of their bows with handkerchiefs at the rehearsals, as a sign of ridicule and protest'.

Style and Idea

Form in music can be many specific things, but basically it is the integration of contrasts. This often means the reconciling of diverse and seemingly unrelated material by means of minute touches and instinctive treatment; and the result may be a satisfying, meaningful whole. In La Mer Debussy triumphantly achieved this kind of integration, and the work can be regarded as 'absolute music': whether it represents the sea or the countryside of Burgundy is quite incidental – and, judging by one of the composer's letters, Debussy too may well have regarded this as incidental. The important thing is that an *essentially mosaic* structure is given an overall design and purpose. In La Mer this comes about in an original way, with (as we have shown) a condensed form of syntax, especially evident in the second movement, and with orchestral colouring vital to the musical sense.

Debussy's style amounts to a radical and extremely sensitive approach to harmony, melody, rhythm, form, seeking a fluidity and freedom (but never without discipline), in direct and sensual contact with the material of sound, sensing the meaning of the passing moment – working outwards from the passing moment. At first he was reacting against German romanticism and following Gounod and Massenet in the cultivation of a truly French style which was lyrical, elegant, leavened by lightness of spirit. His originality in the early songs, for example, is seen first through a widening of key-range and subtle irregular grouping of bars. The Russian influence, church modes, the polyphony of Lassus heard in Rome, oriental music heard in Paris, the Spanish folk-song collection of Pedrell – the influence of such things can be found in a modality of melody and harmony, the development of exotic elements in his style, and a cultivation of improvisatory, arabesque-like writing (a music which 'should not seem to be written down'). Add to this the great enriching influence of Wagner, whose chromatic harmony changed the logic and constructive power of tonality in ways which affected Debussy as much as they affected Bruckner and Mahler (though the results were very different). Schoenberg has written: 'One of the consequences was the so-called impressionistic use of harmonies, especially practised by Debussy. His harmonies, without constructive meaning, often served the colouristic purpose of expressing moods and pictures. Moods and pictures, though extra-musical, thus become constructive elements, incorporated in the musical functions; they produced a sort of emotional comprehensibility.'[1]

When Schoenberg said 'without constructive meaning' he was juxtaposing Debussy's methods with the traditional system of *tonal* contrast inherent in classical and romantic design. But Debussy's musical constructions in fact have a logic and character of their own, completely justifiable in purely musical terms, whatever their extra-musical associations of 'moods and pictures'. Tonality was extended, the feeling for key made more fluid – through modality, rapid and frequent modulation, a flexibility of style akin to improvisation (but never losing the feeling of purpose), and an exploration of textures and timbres. All this was frequently reflected, too, in irregular bar-grouping and irregular rhythms. A free association of ideas had to be unified. Personal harmonic characteristics included the use of the sharpened fourth and flattened seventh of the scale. Chords of the ninth came to be regarded as concords, as points of repose after more dissonant

[1] Arnold Schoenberg, *Style and Idea* (New York and London, 1951).

harmony. Besides *Tristan*, Wagner's *Parsifal* had in many ways a very precise influence on Debussy: it clarified his ideas on the blending of orchestral colours (as it did also for Stravinsky in his early career), on the use of decorations, inner syncopations, pedal notes – and many specific effects, such as high, ethereal chords. We have mentioned also the Javanese gamelan, with its rich and impersonal percussive quality, so often reflected in Debussy's piano writing – and hence in his orchestral textures, for from about the time of *La Mer* piano and orchestra became equally important media for the expression of the full range of his musical imagination.

Le style, c'est l'homme – the aphorism known to every Frenchman – is an untruth. Not style alone, but style inseparably linked with idea makes the man. Through self-expression, the creative artist conveys to others his sense of values (with which we may or may not be in sympathy). With the composer, this may be in purely musical and aesthetic terms, or it may be part of a more widely-embracing vision. A composer such as Michael Tippett sees his art in the context of all the most basic social problems of his time. Debussy, in the romantic tradition of Berlioz and Liszt, could find the initial creative impulse in painting, sculpture, poetry, literature, music – all being part of an extremely sensitive, hedonistic, here-and-now world-picture which he shared with his intimate friend, the writer Pierre Louÿs; and whatever the impulses and associations, the resultant music always contains its meaning in itself. He was fully aware of the problems of creating large-scale musical forms without resorting to ready-made formulas. All his life he detested academic rules and guide-lines. This was something of an obsession – to such an extent that it was impossible for him to write a straightforward, unadorned perfect cadence. And he always strove never to repeat himself. 'One's technique must be constructed afresh', he said, 'according to the demands of each work.' Stravinsky felt the same: in each work, he said, he renewed himself in spirit. Similarly Picasso: 'Every time I begin a picture, I feel as though I'm throwing myself into a void.'

Images

With such thoughts in mind, we can perhaps see the next important orchestral work by Debussy in its true light. It was characteristic of him that after the achievement of *La Mer* he had to go on towards regions unexplored – to increase the range of things translatable into music. In *Images* (which, incidentally, is quite distinct from the two sets of *Images* for piano) Debussy said he was seeking 'an effect of reality'; it was a music 'made up of colours and rhythms', but with a far greater variety of textures and a wider lyrical expansion than in any of his previous works. There is certainly no falling-off in technique: the composer was at the height of his powers – as he also showed himself to be in the later *Jeux*. The emotional range, too, is extended: we feel strongly the personality of the composer in the centre, but in a broad, universal context, symbolised by the exploration of the spirit of three different countries – England, Spain and France. Folk-song, or quasi-folk-material, was used, including 'The Keel Row' in *Gigues,* and two French tunes in *Rondes de Printemps,* partly in a directly evocative and picturesque way, but at the same time completely integrated and often infused with a meaning beyond its original nature. The outward 'reality' is combined with the inner world of the composer's imagination. There is nothing limited or mannered or 'arty' about this work: all that is best and most profoundly exploratory in Debussy's art comes together here with superb mastery and self-realisation.

The range of orchestral colour is larger than Debussy had previously employed. The total orchestra for *Images* is: two piccolos, two flutes, two oboes, oboe d'amore, cor anglais, three clarinets, bass clarinet, three bassoons, double bassoon, four horns, four trumpets, three trombones, tuba, timpani, cymbals, side drum, tambourine, castanets, xylophone, celesta, bells, two harps and the normal strings. And yet, ironically, the movements *Ibéria* and *Rondes de Printemps* were originally intended as works for two pianos, and announced as such in 1905, the year that *La Mer* was first performed; and *Gigues* was originally completed in a piano-duet version. By 1906, however, Debussy was promising his publisher the set of three pieces, in orchestral form, by the end of that year. As it turned out, he was distracted by other work, including the projected opera based on Edgar Allan Poe's *The Fall of the House of Usher*, and the completion of the three orchestral *Images* was considerably delayed. The order of composition was *Ibéria* (1906–8), *Rondes de Printemps* (1908–9), and *Gigues* (1909–12), and each had a separate first performance. Though conceived as a unity, each movement can, if we wish, be regarded as an entity in itself, detachable from the rest: there is no direct musical relationship between them. Of the three, the best known is *Ibéria*, frequently performed separately; and as this is itself divided into three 'movements', a further feeling of completeness is provided.

NO. I – GIGUES

Although this was the last of the three in composition and performance, Debussy published *Gigues* as No. 1 of *Images*. The title was originally *Gigues tristes* – a contradiction in terms (the *gigue* being in origin a lively English dance in triple rhythm) but nevertheless conveying perfectly the ambiguous mood of the piece. The character of the music has been subjectively described by André Caplet (the composer and conductor who helped Debussy with the job of scoring *Gigues*): 'A soul in pain . . . a wounded soul . . . Underneath the convulsive shudderings, the sudden efforts at restraint, the pitiful grimaces, which serve as a kind of disguise, we recognise . . . the spirit of sadness, infinite sadness . . .'[1]

The spirit of sadness is emphasised by the use of the plaintive oboe d'amore for the first of the two principal themes. I have tried, through the English Folk Song and Dance Society, to trace a definite folk-tune which Debussy had in mind – or which he may have remembered wrongly; but no such tune, it seems, can be found. The folk-song expert A. L. Lloyd finds it a good imitation, and has commented:[2] 'Debussy had excellent intuitions regarding such matters. The final phrase is a commonplace of British (and general European) folklore – 'The Drunken Sailor', 'Cock of the North', etc. – but there Debussy may have been prompted by his fancy for pentatonic phrases.'

Ex. 17

Oboe d'amore

[1] Quoted in Lockspeiser, *op. cit.*
[2] In a letter to the author (30 January 1974).

'Convulsive shudderings' is a justifiable subjective reaction to Debussy's somewhat grotesque transformation of 'The Keel Row', a dance song closely associated with the Tyneside district. It appears that Debussy's first inspiration for this piece may have been a poem by Verlaine, entitled *Streets*. It begins:

> J'aimais surtout ses jolies yeux,
> Plus clairs que l'étoile des cieux,
> J'aimais ses yeux malicieux.
> Dansons la gigue!

Verlaine is said to have written this poem in London, in a Soho café at the corner of Old Compton Street and Greek Street. In 1890 Charles Bordes, conductor of the Chanteurs de Saint Gervais in Paris, had set the poem as a song, under the title *Dansons la gigue*, to the tune of 'The Keel Row' – and this would have been known to Debussy.

How much André Caplet contributed to the final musical result we do not know. He had been friendly with Debussy from 1907 and completed the orchestration of several of his works, including *Gigues*. As a composer he was much influenced by Debussy and in general sympathy with his work. Most probably Debussy would have indicated fairly completely in the piano-duet version how he wanted the music orchestrated, and Caplet would have acted simply as an understanding amanuensis.

England had meant quite a lot to Debussy. He may have visited London as early as 1887. Certainly he was there in 1902, at the invitation of André Messager. He completed the scoring of *La Mer* in 1905 at a hotel in Eastbourne, where he had fled with Emma Bardac after the scandal of his wife's attempted suicide. He conducted *L'Après-midi* and *La Mer* at Queen's Hall in 1908, and came to London again the following year to conduct *L'Après-midi* and *Fêtes,* returning later the same year to supervise rehearsals of *Pelléas et Mélisande* at Covent Garden. Two singers in particular, Maggie Teyte and Mary Garden, were very understandingly attuned to his music. Over all, there was far more personal alliance with England than with Spain (but Spain was a dream-world – of which more later).

The introduction of *Gigues,* with divided strings playing harmonics, harp *glissandi*, a soft roll on the cymbals, might suggest a misty Monet-like landscape. Against this the first flute has a whole-tone figure based on the opening notes of 'The Keel Row', leading to the first main theme, *doux et mélancolique,* played by the oboe d'amore (Ex. 17). Soon the rhythm becomes dance-like, and the woodwind have a modified and rather sinister version of 'The Keel Row'. The piece consists of a contrasting and blending of these two tunes in a fairly straightforward manner. About half-way through (at figure 10 in the score) the oboe d'amore begins another expressive melody which seems to have developed as a counter-melody to an obsessive rhythmic pattern in the strings, derived from a section of 'The Keel Row'. This becomes important in the development. A striking and oddly-scored climax effect is achieved by a single *sforzando* high note, given to two piccolos and a solo violin (playing in artificial harmonics), combining with a cymbal roll (executed with timpani sticks) – before a rapid *diminuendo* and a return to the atmosphere of the introduction and first oboe d'amore section ... On the whole, a strange and haunting piece, combining beauty, melancholy and the grotesque in a disturbing but certainly meaningful way.

NO. 2 – IBÉRIA

Many nineteenth- and twentieth-century composers have felt the attraction of the vivid colours and rhythms of Spain, and this has been reflected in their work: for example, Liszt's *Spanish Rhapsody,* Glinka's *Jota Aragonesa* and *Night in Madrid,* Rimsky-Korsakov's *Capriccio espagnol,* Chabrier's *España,* Lalo's *Symphonie espagnole* (written for the Spanish violinist Sarasate), Bizet's *Carmen,* Ravel's *Alborada del gracioso* and the opera *L'Heure espagnole,* and (in satirical vein) pieces by Lord Berners and Walton. French composers have been particularly keen to include elements from the other side of the Pyrenees. In most cases it has been simply a surface take-over of some of the superficial characteristics of Spanish popular music – polos, habaneras, madrileñas, jotas and so on. But the case of Debussy is different.

Although Debussy crossed the Franco-Spanish frontier only once, spending a few hours in San Sebastián (where he watched a bull-fight), he was able to write music such as *Soirée dans Grenade* (1903) of which Manuel de Falla said: 'The entire piece down to the smallest detail makes one feel the character of Spain.'[1] And Professor J. B. Trend, in his biography of Falla,[2] goes so far as to

[1] 'Le tombeau de Debussy', *La Revue Musicale,* Paris, December 1920.
[2] J. B. Trend, *Manuel de Falla and Spanish Music* (London, 1929).

state that 'it was Debussy who revealed things in the spirit of Andalusian music which had been hidden or not clearly discerned even by Falla, who was born and bred in Andalusia'. When Debussy was composing *Ibéria*, between 1906 and 1908, he became acquainted with Book I of Albéniz's cycle of piano pieces, *Iberia*; he knew also the Spanish folk-song collections of Felipe Pedrell. He must also have felt a natural affinity with Spanish music – to such an extent that he could absorb and assimilate the Spanish characteristics so completely that they became a natural part of his own style. The themes which Debussy uses in *Ibéria* are not borrowed from Spanish folklore, but original material 'in the spirit of' Spanish music. His imagination had been stimulated by singers, players and dancers from Seville and Granada who visited Paris – giving performances of *cante* and *baile jondo* (the name given to a type of Andalusian songs and dances, modal, highly decorated, in many ways quasi-oriental in style and structure). Not only was Debussy affected by the music of Spain, but he himself had an influence on the course of Spanish music. Manuel de Falla found that the turning-point in his own career was his visit to Paris in 1907 and his meeting with Debussy. At the time, the problem of Spanish music was its composers' difficulty in finding satisfactory larger-scale forms in which their particular type of folk-material could be used without irrelevance or loss of identity. Debussy, in *Soirée dans Grenade,* had not only provided a practical solution, but the so-called 'impressionistic' style, the freedom from traditional moulds, seemed to open up possible ways for future developments in Spanish music. 'The evocative nature of *Soirée dans Grenade*', wrote Falla, 'is nothing less than miraculous when one reflects on the fact that this music was written by a foreigner guided almost entirely by his visionary genius.'[1] In *Ibéria,* Debussy went much deeper. He did not, according to Falla, intend to write Spanish music, but rather 'to translate into music the associations that Spain had aroused in him'. This, Falla concludes, he triumphantly did. The effect which Debussy's *Ibéria* had on Falla must have been overwhelming, providing him with examples difficult to match in quality. His own *Four Spanish Pieces,* which were published the following year in Paris, are pleasant, but tame by comparison. It was not until 1916 that *Nights in the Gardens of Spain* appeared, establishing Falla's personality as a composer –

[1] Falla, *op. cit.*

but the debt to Debussy is still immense, in technique and in the kind of evocation aimed at in this music.

Debussy's *Ibéria* is divided into three contrasted sections, with distinct titles, representing village music-making in the bright glare of midday, the heavy perfumes of a summer night in Andalusia, and a crescendo of merry-making on the morning of a public holiday.

(i) *Par les rues et par les chemins* (In the highways and byways). At once it becomes clear that Debussy is (in Falla's phrase) writing music not *a la española* (in the Spanish manner) but *en español* (in Spanish). He is also using his complete range of harmonic and rhythmic subtlety, and richly-coloured, sensitive orchestral textures. We are plunged at once (as we were in *Fêtes*) into one of Debussy's 'cosmic' rhythms, pointed with castanets and tambourine. The generic theme, given out by clarinets, is a kind of *sevillana,* and suggested to Falla 'village songs heard in the bright, scintillating light'.

Ex. 18

Most of the abundant melodic and rhythmic material of the movement derives from this fragment. The second bar contains an overworked but typical Spanish melodic cliché, but we are never aware of anything obvious in Debussy's treatment. If we think of bars 4 and 5 together, they suggest the characteristic ambiguity between 6/8 and 3/4 time in Spanish music – a feeling which Debussy subtly exploits in this movement. One thematic variant is:

Ex. 19

Melodic phrases are constantly passed from one group of instruments to another in a joyous and finely controlled diversity. Oboe and viola have a contrasted theme which feels like an extension of Ex. 19, and is heard also in the *Parfums de la nuit* section:

Ex. 20

Horns lead off an intrusive rhythmic variant in march time, which is developed (with some counter-melodies) by the whole orchestra. Towards the end, the main theme returns, in a new treatment, and after one more emphatic statement the music gradually disperses, rather as it did at the end of *Fêtes*.

(ii) *Les Parfums de la nuit*. The intoxicating fragrance of the Andalusian night is portrayed in a dreamlike atmosphere, but with detailed precision. Against a shimmering background, the oboe presents, whole-tonally, an expressive *habanera* theme. Rippling woodwind, and *glissandi* chords in the strings, do not disturb the sensitive languor in which fragments of themes come and go. Divided violas and cellos take up the *habanera* rhythm, while the oboe has a version of Ex. 20, from the previous movement; then the whole body of strings, much divided, has a rich chordal version of the rhythmic pattern. The contrast comes, in true *habanera* style, with a sudden passionate upthrust in the strings. At first this is intermittent, then (in thirds) becomes animated and increases in intensity, reaching an expressive climax and subsiding. The fragments of lingering melody become a transition passage of magical subtlety. Superimposed on two bars of whole-tone texture in strings and horns, distant bells and muted trumpet hint at the rhythmic and joyous music that is to follow, without a break, in the next section.

(iii) *Le Matin d'un jour de fête*. Light-hearted holiday crowds beginning a day of endless festivity. Debussy said of this section: 'It sounds like music which has not been written down! The whole rising feeling, the awakening of people and of nature. There is a water-melon vendor and children whistling – I see them all clearly.' So vivid was his imagination – though he did not know Spain. In structure the movement often suggests improvised music-making 'which has not been written down'. Yet how precisely Debussy *has* written it all down! The sounds and the rhythms of the accumulating festivities, with tambourine, side-drum and bells adding irregularly to the animation, with fragments of song and dance appearing and disappearing – memories, sometimes parodied, from the previous sections – the whole thing taking on a march-like musical shape. Such, roughly, is the impression of the first part. We have a glimpse (reappearing later) of dancing to a strumming on the guitar. The violins and violas of the orchestra are instructed to hold their instruments under the arm like a guitar and to strum in chords, which eventually become clear and emphatic:

Falla tells us that Spanish composers have neglected and even despised such effects: they considered them primitive. It was Debussy, he said, who showed how such effects could be used with imagination.

Over further strumming a raucous clarinet (the direct ancestor of the one in Copland's *El Salón México*) rends the festive air. Soon a solitary strolling fiddler is heard, and rudely interrupted before he has got further than one phrase. (In this part of the work we can hear presentiments of Stravinsky's *Petrushka* and *The Soldier's*

Tale.) Oboe and cor anglais pick up the fiddler's melody, and the development becomes animated, building to an excited climax (*vif et nerveux*) in a whirl of dancing.

NO. 3 – RONDES DE PRINTEMPS

'The music has this about it,' Debussy said, apropos of this movement of *Images*, 'it is elusive, and consequently cannot be handled like a robust symphony which walks on all fours (sometimes on threes, but walks nevertheless).' When Debussy conducted the first performance of this music in 1910 at the Concerts Durand in Paris, a programme note, which may have represented the composer's views, likened its style to the multiplicity of lines in a drawing, and the orchestra to a huge palette wherein each instrument contributes its particular colour. The *Rondes de Printemps,* even more than the other movements of *Images,* is a highly personal expression of the composer's unique vision, with a characteristic underlying melancholy pervading the music – the *lacrimae rerum* – belying the lighthearted quotation at the beginning of the score.

> Vive le mai, bienvenu soit le mai
> Avec son gonfalon sauvage!
> (Long live May! Welcome May,
> with its rustic banner!)

Debussy had come across the quotation in a book, *Dante,* by Pierre Gauthiez, published in 1908, the year *Rondes de Printemps* was begun. The lines are a French translation of part of one of the *Canzoni a ballo* by a fifteenth-century Italian humanist, Politian, and are used by Gauthiez as part of a description of medieval May-Day celebrations in Tuscany. Women and girls, garlanded with flowers, form processions and pair off with joyous dancers and musicians. The whole countryside is alive and rejoicing. But in his copy of Gauthiez's *Dante* Debussy also marked a *Ballata* by Guido Cavalcanti, written when the poet was in exile and occupied with thoughts of his approaching death. In January 1909, four months before he completed the score of *Rondes de Printemps,* Debussy had the first signs of the cancer which within ten years was to cause his death.

The emotion conveyed in this piece is consistently ambiguous. One or two bars occasionally break through to an unclouded major key, but they are very brief moments in an otherwise complex texture in which the simple, gay French tune 'Nous

n'irons plus au bois' (Ex. 22a) is heard – the first part of it –
shaped and harmonically transformed into something quite unlike its original self (b) – as also happened to 'The Keel Row' in
Gigues. Augmented versions of this phrase are also important in the
music's structure, played in long notes of equal length (c).

Ex. 22

(a)

Nous n'i – rons plus au bois; les lau-riers sont cou – pés

(b) (♩= 126)

p

gracieux et gaiement

(c) (♩= 126)

It was the third time Debussy had used this French tune in his
works (in more obvious forms it was also heard in the song 'La
Belle au bois dormant' and the piano piece *Jardins sous la pluie*).
There are also some rather heavily camouflaged references to the
first notes of the nursery song 'Do, do, l'enfant do.'

Essentially, *Rondes de Printemps* is a complex evocative piece, a
personal image of spring and the reawakening of nature in a
French setting, produced by minute touches (the simile of *pointil-
lisme* in painting is appropriate) – the phrases are short, the colour
effects ever-varying, and textures are fragmented. Everything in
fact is rapidly changing the whole time. Musically, it directly
foreshadows parts of Stravinsky's *Rite of Spring* which are similar
in purpose, and in technique very indebted. Debussy's opening
pages of *Rondes de Printemps* are a miracle of delicate, intricate
scoring: tremolo strings, harmonics, high shimmering chords,
fragmentary chromatic phrases, suggestions of folk-song, harp
glissandi, string *glissandi* – all contribute to an impression of the
uneasy awakening of the natural world, in preparation for the
dance, *léger et fantasque,* which soon establishes itself in an irregular
5-pulse rhythm (15/8). This, however, soon gives way to another
intricate section which again seems to be representative of the
sounds of nature, with effects of colour and rhythm rather than
any clearly-defined themes. The dance begins afresh with more

definite purpose, and is developed in a variety of forms. Rhythmically the structure is complex, but the overall shape comes from the
different treatments of the main theme (Ex. 22b), interspersed
with episodic material, and the 5-pulse dance-rhythm is heard
again. At the climax, *joyeux,* in a clear A major, the background
rhythm has become identical with the rhythm of the opening of
Fêtes (Ex. 9); but this is short-lived.

Ritual and Personality

The kind of things written about the *Rondes de Printemps* when it
first appeared are typical of the controversial atmosphere which
normally surrounded the important works of Debussy. Ravel, who
did not normally break into musical criticism, referred – in the
Cahiers d'aujourd'hui – to the *charme éclatant* and the *fraîcheur
exquise* (vivid charm and exquisite freshness) of this movement of
Images, and he sarcastically took to task the Parisian critic Gaston
Carraud, who (not without careful thought) considered the music
to be based on artificial technical processes rather than emotional
feeling, and who found the style less concise, more cumbersome,
the method of construction more visible, more studied, than in the
composer's earlier style. Another writer, Louis Laloy, a friend and
advocate of Debussy, found that certainly the style had changed,
but had become more substantial than the older form of *Debus-
sysme.* At the time many (perhaps most) musicians were finding
Debussy's music a bitter fruit in which dissonance had become the
rule – in other words, a far-fetched and disturbing kind of experience. Today, when the *Rite of Spring* is accepted as a classic,
when the norm of acceptable assault and battery is completely
different, and when disintegration is carried to extremes as a matter
of course, it is very difficult for us to appreciate the effect that the
major works of Debussy had at the time of their first appearance.
One of the basic differences in effect – afterwards exploited by
other composers, and now a process which seems quite natural –
was to distribute the harmonic textures throughout the whole
orchestra, rather than keeping them to clear-cut groups of instruments; likewise also to vary the thematic material, the *motifs,* by
constantly passing them to different levels – to different tone-
colours. Above all, the orchestra, in the mature Debussy works,

has been likened to a 'stylised gamelan', a kind of impersonal, ritualised means of expression, with something of the collective extemporised effect of the Javanese gamelan which impressed Debussy so much when he heard it.

To understand the nature of this, we must briefly consider two very different kinds of musical expression, which can be called, for convenience, ritual and personality. Going back as far as possible, art for the savage is in the nature of an act of propitiation, an offering to the gods, part of the process of coming to terms with forces that are feared and not understood. Art is a ritual act linked first with immediate necessity, and unreflective; later, when the ritual continues to be performed, without immediate necessity, there is time for reflection and even enjoyment: the scope of the offering expands, the ritual produces an emotion in those present, a particular state of mind is induced . . . In some such way art must have come into being and developed. Dance, the art of gesture, was vitally connected with religion and ritual in ancient Greece and Rome, in Indian as in Japanese temples. The measured gestures of the dance are bound up with rhythm – rhythm, which is the basic source of musical expression . . . Reflecting on the *nature* of the ritual offering, with care and skill producing as fine an offering as possible, patterns and textures are made more elaborate, and through choice of material comes an aesthetic quality, but individual personality is still submerged. Impersonality, in this sense, and a ritual quality are found in plainsong, in polyphonic church music, and in the work of many composers, including Stravinsky. Stravinsky has described himself as an objectivist, a constructive artist. He rejected expressiveness as a conscious aim (as medieval composers did). He believed that 'music is, by its very nature, essentially powerless to express anything at all, whether a feeling, an attitude of mind, a psychological mood, a phenomenon of nature'. Even the idea of a solemn pagan fertility ceremony (which led to the composing of *The Rite of Spring*) was in theory only a pretext for music which was always 'objective' – akin to the so-called 'abstract' painters (such as the Fauves and the Cubists) who sought to achieve 'pure' works of art by formal means which did not depend on representation of nature or subjective associations. Stravinsky also stated that music is 'the sole domain in which man realises the present', and that music exists to establish an order between Man and Time. His aim in music was therefore closely parallel to the equally definite aims of the painters Matisse and Braque, who sought to reconcile man to his existence by means of aesthetic forms.

At the other extreme we have the romantic, *self-expressive* composer – for example, Beethoven, Berlioz, Schumann, Mahler. And, a very clear example, Arnold Bax, who said quite unambiguously: 'My music is the expression of emotional states; I have no interest whatever in sound for its own sake.'

Debussy – starting in romantic style, then reacting against overblown nineteenth-century romanticism – arrived at a more impersonal, ritualistic form of composition. Instead of the personal feelings of the artist being the most important part of the message, we have an art where a sense of values is differently conveyed – where a work is objectively prepared, elaborated, perfected, and is then presented for contemplation by others as something of significance in itself, through its own form and qualities.

The best way to give an impression of Debussy's sensitive and imaginative orchestral style is by quoting a characteristic ten bars from a mature work. Ex. 23 is from the *Rondes de Printemps*. Here we can see the delicacy and precision with which the details of the colourful scoring are carried out, the meticulous care in marking the exact expression in all the different instruments, the knowledge of what is most effective for each. To have much-divided strings was a favourite device of the composer, as was the temporary changing of tone-colour by marking the violas and cellos to play *sur la touche* (over the fingerboard, where the tone is mellower). Note also how, in building up to a climax, the woodwind tone becomes reinforced at a certain point by *pizzicato* strings. Again, the textures of trilled and *tremolando* strings (in the last three bars) forming a background to the melodic strands in the woodwind, combined with a softly beaten cymbal, are very characteristic. A particularly beautiful detail, in the third and fourth bars, is the delicate percussive effect of the two harps, the second one playing in artificial harmonics, duplicating between them the melody of the solo flute. We can see, too, how the harmonic importance passes from strings to wind, and then back to strings.

Ex. 23

48

Jeux

The last orchestral work of Debussy, the *poème dansé*, *Jeux*, comes nearest to his long-wished-for ideal of a flexible music which seems not to be written down, a freedom of musical speech, ever-varying in colours, shapes, rhythms. The musical adventurousness and radical importance of *Jeux* were overshadowed at the time of its first performance (May 1913) by another very important work, Stravinsky's *Rite of Spring*, which appeared at almost exactly the same time and with its sensational impact stole all the thunder. After many years of neglect, *Jeux* has comparatively recently come to be regarded as a key work in twentieth-century music. Previously, it was considered merely elusive and indefinite – which certainly it is not. Outwardly the style was not sensational or revolutionary, but followed directly from Debussy's previous lines of development. The advance was in the degree and clarity of its free form, the attitude to thematic material, structure, orchestral textures, timbres, rhythm – an outlook and technique which directly foreshadowed later 'avant-garde' procedures. *Jeux* is a direct extension of the style of writing which was displayed in the second movement of *La Mer*, 'Jeu de vagues': the rapidly-shifting textures, changing too quickly for traditional 'development', becoming fragmented and decorative, a play of timbres – an extraordinary example of subtle modulation in harmonic, rhythmic and melodic terms.

But what were the circumstances of its composition? The scandal of Nijinsky's version of the *Prélude à l'Après-midi d'un Faune* for Diaghilev's Russian Ballet was still in people's minds. Diaghilev had the idea of another sensational ballet, this time on a simple, 'realistic' contemporary theme – something new and revolutionary in ballet – with choreography by Nijinsky in which he could exploit his new-found style of dancing, called 'stylised gesture'; and Debussy would be commissioned to compose the music. According to what Nijinsky wrote in his diary, Diaghilev (who was a homosexual) originally wanted the 'story' to be about three young men making love to each other. That, however, would have caused too much of a scandal, even for him. So the idea then changed to two girls and a boy, a game of tennis with amorous side-play, interrupted by the crashing of an aeroplane. Debussy was approached; but at first he turned the idea down.

'No, it's idiotic and unmusical! I would not dream of writing the score.' His fee was doubled; there was pleading and modification. The aeroplane was taken out. In the end, the idea, with its combination of simplicity and undertones, seemed to appeal to Debussy. On the day of the first performance of *Jeux* (at the Théâtre des Champs-Elysées, Paris, on 15 May 1913) an article by the composer was published in which he spoke of 'a scenario made of that subtle *rien du tout* of which I think the story of a ballet should be composed'. The scenario had become 'a park, a game of tennis, the chance encounter of two girls and a young man in pursuit of a lost tennis ball, a mysterious nocturnal landscape, with that slightly naughty, indefinable something sheltered by the shadows; leaps, turns, capricious steps, all that is necessary to bring rhythm to birth in a musical atmosphere'. Writing to his publisher, he had expressed some doubts about the music having to make a rather *risqué* situation acceptable. But he added: 'Where ballet is concerned, immorality escapes through the dancers' legs and ends in a pirouette.'

In the end, Debussy hated Nijinsky's realisation: too literal in some places, totally unrelated in others. And the abstraction and stylised gesture he found ugly. Moreover, the sports got confused, and mirth was caused by having a tennis ball the size of a football, and some of the action seemed to relate to golf, not tennis. When the production of *Jeux* came from Paris to London, with the title changed to *Playtime*, the critic of the *Daily Mail* found the ballet 'disconcerting, delicious and discreetly amusing, as is M. Debussy's music'. And the critic of the *Morning Post* observed: 'The business is conceived in the vein of the Cubists. It is a triumph of angularity. It fits M. Debussy's music very well, and the music is wholly suited to it. . . . The cumulative rhythms – wholly meaningless – are suited with action of similar character. The audience first laughed and then applauded.'

So much for the initial impression, in which the stage action seems to have done much to prevent the music from being taken seriously. Debussy composed the work, however, with the stage action clearly in mind the whole time. Subtle and unconventional though the music is, the organisation of the score was directly and realistically related to the requirements of the scenario. It was Debussy who determined the musical forms for the dancing: Nijinsky then worked out the choreography, in abstract plastic forms and with inspiration from paintings by Gauguin. It was decided that the 'story' should be cyclic: at the end the action was interrupted, not by an incongruous aeroplane, but by another ball falling on the stage. Debussy was prevailed upon to change his ending – to conclude with music similar to the first chordal prelude – thus rounding off the musical form in a manner somewhat reminiscent of his friend Dukas's scherzo, *L'Apprenti Sorcier*.

In a letter to André Caplet, Debussy wrote, apropos of *Jeux:* 'I had to find an orchestration "without feet". Don't imagine I mean an orchestra composed entirely of cripples. No! I'm thinking of that orchestral colouring which seems to be lit from behind and of which there are so many marvellous effects in *Parsifal*.' Debussy's orchestration is clear and direct; and although a large orchestra is used (quadruple woodwind and brass, percussion, celeste, two harps and strings), the textures are on the whole more like those of chamber music, with every instrument seeming to play an important role, and no part where all the instruments are playing together. Even at the climaxes, the use of instruments is carefully selective. The short melodic and rhythmic *motifs* are distributed and varied in orchestral treatment until it feels as though a whole self-contained world of timbres has been created. The intensity of a phrase depends both on dynamic marks and on the way it is orchestrated, and there are constantly special colour-markings such as 'col legno', 'flautando', 'sur la touche', 'près de la table' (for the harp), and so on.

That is the colour side of the work, which is of immense richness and variety. The same is true of the other aspects of the score. The unrestricted resources of diatonism and chromaticism are employed. Only in the prelude and postlude is there a purely whole-tone passage; and very rarely is there a pentatonic suggestion. Occasionally, polytonal effects are produced, but always with a basic harmonic justification. Debussy was deliberately writing music that was mobile, fleeting, ever-changing. The flow, the continuity is there, but very difficult to analyse. *Motifs* are linked, appear and disappear – occasionally returning in new forms. At times rondo shape is vaguely suggested, but in fact no traditional form or development is followed: melodic and rhythmic *motifs* are subtly varied in the construction as a whole. Some twenty-three different *motifs* can be counted. One of these can perhaps be called a 'main theme'; it dominates the texture at three points – and fleetingly appears elsewhere four other times:

Ex. 24

No *motif* is ever repeated in the same form twice, and nearly all move in conjunct steps or thirds, and form four- or eight-bar lengths. Sometimes the form of a section is derived from *ostinato*. The harmonic structures have a logic of their own, but are often 'non-functional' in traditional terms. Rhythmically, there is immense subtlety and variety – linked to the stage action, but having great freedom. The basic tempo is of a moderate scherzo (♩. = 72), but this is flexible – constantly modified by a *rubato* feeling which any interpretation of this work must have.

Jeux opens with a slow eight bars, in which, over a long-held B in the strings, the woodwind (*doux et rêveur* – a favourite indication of Debussy's) play various inversions of a whole-tone chord. The first scherzando *motif* (in 3/8) is interrupted by a return of the slow whole-tone idea, in a very different and ornamented version, and this leads to the principal *motif* (Ex. 24). At this point 'the curtain rises on an empty park'. A high *sforzando* chord followed by a falling arpeggio figure marks the arrival of the tennis ball bouncing on to the stage. A young man in tennis clothes, brandishing a racket, bounds across the scene and disappears. Now two girls appear, and their timidity and curiosity are reflected by the tremulous music in the strings and a chromatic rise and fall in the woodwind. They seem to be seeking out a place where they can talk in private. The 'main theme' (Ex. 24) returns and develops in intensity; the first girl dances, then the second – to the same musical idea, but differently orchestrated and continuing differently. Again the main theme returns in a new orchestral guise. The music becomes agitated as the girls are interrupted by the sound of rustling leaves. They see the young man watching them through the branches. He stops them from running away, brings them gently back, and persuades one of them to dance with him. The music becomes a light-hearted waltz, very fluid and *rubato* in feeling, now restless, now sustained and expressive. He asks for a kiss; the girl escapes; he asks again; again she escapes – only to return to him, now consenting. The music reflects the actions, and rises to a brief passionate climax.

The tempo changes to 2/4: the slight jealousy of the second girl is portrayed by muted horn in an ironic passage, and she begins a mocking dance, which the young man follows – at first from curiosity, and then with genuine interest. Abandoning the first girl, he concentrates his attention on the other, teaching her the steps of the dance. At first she responds mockingly, but soon their dance has genuine feeling; but it is interrupted when the girl teasingly escapes and hides. Before long they are dancing again more and more joyously, until the music reaches a wild climax – with a single *sforzando* high B flat, followed by a descending passage in rapid *diminuendo* (a climax very similar to the one near the end of *Gigues*). The abandoned girl has been forgotten. Sadly, she wants to leave. During the more tentative music that follows, her companion tries to hold her back, and eventually takes her in a close embrace. And now the young man intervenes, gently separating their heads. As they gaze around at the beauty of evening, the glow, the happiness – everything encourages them to follow where their fantasy leads them. The *motif* of Ex. 24 again begins a new section, gradually picking up in animation and expressive intensity, and all three join in the dance. The intensity increases to a violent and passionate climax. At the culmination, the young man impetuously unites all three of them in an ecstatic triple kiss. Tension is released, spaciously and expressively, in twelve bars based on the first four notes of Ex. 24. Suddenly, a tennis ball falls at their feet. Alarmed, they run off, disappearing into the depths of the park and the night. We hear a new version of the mysterious whole-tone chords of the first prelude, dissolving into a few final fragmented sounds as the curtain falls.

Debussy had written a score which followed very closely the requirements of a somewhat pretentious scenario. The intention of Nijinsky's ballet had been to provide 'an apologia in plastic terms for the man of 1913'. Despite the collaboration of Léon Bakst for décor and costumes, despite the talents of the dancers Karsavina, Ludmila Schollar and Nijinsky, and of the conductor Pierre Monteux, the ballet as a whole could not be reckoned a success, and it is unlikely to be effectively revived in its original conception. In the concert hall, however, the music has now many times proved that it has a life of its own. It is not likely that *Jeux* will suffer neglect in the future.

. . . et Alia

PRINTEMPS (1887)

The symphonic suite *Printemps* is the earliest orchestral work of Debussy that is known. There was a so-called Symphony in B – written about the end of 1880 – a very immature work, which he sent to Madame Nadezhda von Meck (by whom he had been engaged as pianist) – but this is known only in a version for piano duet; likewise *Le Triomphe de Bacchus* of 1882, which was intended as an orchestral interlude. The *Intermezzo* for orchestra of the same year, based on a poem of Heine, has remained unpublished.

Printemps was written in Rome, early in 1887, and was said to be inspired by Botticelli's famous picture *Primavera*. In fact, the aim of this pantheistic work was quite clearly stated by Debussy in a letter of that time. 'The idea I had was to compose a work of a particular colour which would cover a wide range of feeling. It will be called *Printemps,* not a descriptive Spring but in human terms. I should like to convey the slow and miserable birth of beings and things in nature, their gradual blossoming-out, and finally the joy of being born anew. All this is to be done without a "programme", because I detest all music which follows some literary text one happens to have got hold of.'

The work was one of the 'envois' which, at regular intervals, holders of the Prix de Rome were obliged to send back to Paris to show how they were progressing. The original score, for orchestra and chorus, was accidentally destroyed in a fire at the bookbinders where the composer had sent it. The official report of the Académie des Beaux-Arts had little good to say about the work: it showed too strong a taste for the unusual (*la recherche de l'étrange*). Interesting to note that they found the exaggerated sense of colour made the young composer overlook precision of form and outline; he must be on his guard *contre cet impressionnisme vague* – which they called 'one of the most dangerous enemies of truth in works of art'. They found the first movement confused, and the second bizarre and incoherent. Seven years later, in 1904, it was printed in a version for piano duet and chorus, as a supplement to a musical review. The first performance was not till 1913 – in a purely orchestral version made by Henri Büsser (following Debussy's indications). A full symphony orchestra is used, including a part for harp and a rather crudely 'doubling' part for piano duet. There is no connection between this work and Debussy's earlier Prix de Rome choral exercises, *Printemps* (1882 and 1884), later published as *Salut, Printemps*.

Only occasionally in the orchestral *Printemps* is the style really characteristic of Debussy. (One passage closely resembles part of *L'Après-midi*.) It is the colour, freshness and exuberance which make the work still live for us today. Some of the melodic material is folksong-like in character. The gentle opening melody, on the flute, is heard in different forms in the course of both movements. There is a wide range of feeling in the work, as the composer intended, and the conclusion is splendidly bacchanalian.

Henri Büsser, the conductor and composer, who orchestrated *Printemps*, also made a version for small orchestra of another early work of Debussy – the *Petite Suite* piano duet. Through being much played by many different kinds of light-music ensembles, this has become one of Debussy's most popular works. Edward Lockspeiser has pointed out that each of the four short movements shows a different and distinct French influence important in Debussy's early development. The cool, limpid barcarolle, *En bateau,* owes much to Fauré; the lightly ceremonial flavour of *Cortège* is from Bizet; the classical elegance of the *Menuet* recalls Massenet; and the final *Ballet* seems to combine Chabrier's clarity and verve and the simple appeal of Delibes.

MARCHE ÉCOSSAISE (1891)

Debussy liked this delightful and colourful march, which was written on a Scottish tune. Originally it was for piano duet – worked out with great care and even containing a canon (Debussy may have had Schumann in mind here). The first title was 'Marche des Anciens Comtes de Ross, dédiée à leur descendant, le Général Meredith Reid, Grand Croix de l'Ordre Royal du Rédempteur'. In 1890 Debussy was unexpectedly visited by this distinguished Scottish officer, General Meredith Reid, who spoke no French, but gave Debussy his visiting card. An interpreter had to be hauled out of a nearby tavern before the purpose of the visit could be conveyed: it was a commission to arrange a march-tune traditionally associated with the General's ancestors, the ancient Earls of Ross. The chieftain's band of pipers would play this tune before and during battles, and on high days and holidays. Later Debussy orchestrated the piece and extended the final section.

A full symphony orchestra is used, including cor anglais and harp. The tempo indication 'allegretto scherzando' stresses the lighthearted and non-ceremonial nature of the piece. There is a short introduction, in which the whole-tone flavour might be presaging a strikingly original treatment of the simple melody (such as we had of 'The Keel Row' in *Gigues*) – but this is not the case. In the first section the harmony and general treatment are very much in keeping with the sprightly, straightforward character of the Scottish tune. The slow, meditative version which follows in the next section is exotic in that it strongly recalls the folk-song manner of Russian composers; but the Russian element had early become a natural part of Debussy's musical style. Then the march is resumed, now in a lively 6/8 rhythm (instead of 2/4), increasing in excitement to a climax rhythmically emphasised by *tambour militaire* and a cymbal struck by drum-sticks.

WORKS FOR SAXOPHONE, CLARINET AND ORCHESTRA

Sometimes Debussy accepted commissions and was very reluctant to carry them out. One of these came in 1903 from Mrs Richard J. Hall, President of the Orchestral Club in Boston. She was an aspiring saxophonist and wanted Debussy to write a serious work for her instrument. He was working on *La Mer* at the time; and it was also a period of immense crisis in his personal life. The score of the *Rhapsodie* which he wrote for Mrs Hall was not sent to her until 1905 – and even then it was only for saxophone and piano, and not in as 'finished' a state as one would expect from this composer: there are signs of haste and of hard going. But this is a straightforward work, about ten minutes in length, clear and direct in expression; not specially memorable, but written with an understanding of what sounds effective on that ambiguous instrument, which, though much abused, is capable of genuine expressiveness. It was orchestrated by Roger-Ducasse, about a year after the composer's death, in a way that shows a firm understanding of Debussy's manner of scoring.

The two works with clarinet came later, in 1909 and 1910, and in them we can hear the real Debussy. One was a *Petite Pièce*. The other, the so-called *Première Rhapsodie* – he never wrote a second one – clearly and cleverly explores the expressive and technical possibilities of the clarinet, as it was intended to do. At the time Debussy had been appointed a member of the board of the Paris

Conservatoire, which meant that now and then he had to adjudicate at some of the competitive examinations. He was always fascinated and stimulated by the range and possible tone-colours of the wind instruments, and in 1910 he wrote the two test pieces for the clarinet candidates. This *Rhapsodie* and the *Petite Pièce* were both originally for clarinet and piano, and were later orchestrated by Debussy himself. Of the clarinet *Rhapsodie* he once remarked: 'This piece is among the most pleasant I have ever written'.

DANSES (1904) FOR HARP AND STRINGS
(1) *Danse sacrée*   (2) *Danse profane*

The harp is one of the most ancient and universal of musical instruments: strings of different lengths stretched over a frame and plucked by the fingers. The variety is infinite (on earth, and no doubt in heaven too); but with the modern solo and orchestral instrument, the strings are tuned according to the notes of the diatonic major scale. There are seven pedals, each with two notches. With one of these pedals all the Cs of the instrument can be made flat, natural or sharp; with the next all the Ds; and so on – one pedal for each note of the scale. There is also a kind of harp which requires no pedals – the Chromatic Harp – with a separate string for every semitone throughout its range; therefore nearly double the number of strings. It was introduced in 1897 by the firm of Pleyel in Paris.

In 1904, at the invitation of Pleyel, Debussy was asked to write something as a test piece for the chromatic harp, for use at the Brussels Conservatoire. The result was the well-known *Danses* for harp and string orchestra. The writing for the harp is straightforward and effective – not particularly difficult; and they are now usually played on the normal orchestral instrument, not the chromatic harp. The first of the two dances, *Danse sacrée*, is slow, ritualistic, modal in style (reflecting the instrument's antiquity). According to the conductor Ernest Ansermet, this movement was suggested by a piano piece of a friend of Debussy, the Portuguese composer and conductor Francisco de Lacerda; but it seems probable also that a strong influence was the modal and ancient flavour of Erik Satie's haunting *Gymnopédies* (which Debussy liked so much that he made an orchestral version of two of them). In complete contrast, the second movement, *Danse profane*, moves in a lilting waltz rhythm, basically in D major, but characteristically using the sharpened fourth and flattened seventh of the scale. Both movements are rich in modulation.

The title sometimes appears, understandably, as *Danse sacrée et Danse profane*. This was not, however, given by Debussy, who simply used the collective title *Danses*.

INCIDENTAL MUSIC FOR 'KING LEAR'

Debussy, like Berlioz and many other composers, was strongly drawn to Shakespeare. He found Hamlet a particularly fascinating character; early in his career, also, he considered writing music for a version of *As you like it*. In 1904, the actor André Antoine, director of the Théâtre Libre, sought his collaboration for a production of *King Lear*. Owing to other commitments this idea was not fulfilled, but some sketches were made, and these were found among Debussy's manuscripts after his death. Two pieces were edited by Roger-Ducasse in 1926: *Fanfare d'ouverture* (three trumpets, four horns, two harps, timpani and tabor) consists of eighteen bars of majestic scene-setting, presumably before the action that takes place in the state-room of King Lear's palace. *Sommeil de Lear* ('The King's repose') was found fully scored by Debussy for two flutes, four horns, one harp, timpani and strings; it was probably intended as a kind of 'Dead March' at the end.

LE MARTYRE DE SAINT-SÉBASTIEN: SYMPHONIC FRAGMENTS

With the collaboration of his friend and musical disciple André Caplet, a suite of four 'symphonic fragments', for full orchestra, was made from the incidental music which Debussy wrote for the mystery play *Le Martyre de Saint-Sébastien,* by the exiled Italian poet Gabriele d'Annunzio. As originally produced in Paris in 1911, the play (in five acts) was a collaboration between d'Annunzio, Debussy, the dancer Ida Rubinstein, the choreographer Michel Fokine and the painter Léon Bakst. The music was for soloists, chorus and orchestra, written in great haste, but with a sure instinct for conveying or underlining the moods and tensions of the drama. Partly through interference from the Catholic Church, the initial production was not a success. Other forms of it were tried later, including the one that is probably the most satisfactory – as an oratorio and with not too much narrative. The recording (for example) made under Ernest Ansermet in that form is an impressive experience. The music, however, is diffuse in style and lacking in real continuity, but there are pages of originality and boldness where the real Debussy comes to the fore. The composer was attracted to the subject partly because it was, for him, exploring musically a new area of experience, with memories of *Parsifal* in the background; also the approach, which was a blending of Christian and pagan symbolism, would have been congenial. On the religious side Debussy made his position quite clear. 'Even if I am not a practising Catholic nor a believer,' he wrote just before the first performance, 'it did not require much effort on my part to realise what mystical heights the poet's drama reaches.' Elsewhere he wrote: 'I have made mysterious Nature my religion. . . . To feel the supreme and moving beauty of the spectacle which Nature offers to her fleeting guests – that is what I call prayer.'

Undoubtedly the voices (soloists and chorus) are essential for an adequate representation of this music, and the most memorable parts are in fact certain vocal sections. The version arranged for orchestra alone of the sections which form this suite from *The Martyrdom of St Sebastian* is not always self-sufficient as music in its own right. The first fragment, 'The Court of Lilies', begins with a solemn, liturgical-like prelude composed of successions of parallel common chords (an extension of the same idea found in the last part of *La Cathédrale engloutie*). The Roman scene is set for the martyrdom of two young Christians. The richly melodic style is *expressif et douloureux*. In the second section, also from Act I, the 'Ecstatic Dance' of Sebastian on burning embers, in self-punishment, is certainly the most striking and interesting part musically; scored with immense colour and variety, it is both fierce and sensitive in expression. The end of this section is the music accompanying a miracle and a vision of heaven. The poignant music of 'The Passion', which follows, is connected with Sebastian's masochistic expectation of martyrdom at the hands of Caesar. Sebastian welcomes the arrows with the words 'I am the target; from the depths I call forth your terrible love'. The final section, 'The Good Shepherd', comes from Act 4: the music is at its most suggestive and atmospheric, accompanying a scene among the ancient laurels of Apollo's Grove when the saint has a brief vision of the Shepherd and a sacrificial lamb.

KHAMMA – LÉGENDE DANSÉE

In 1911 Debussy was asked by the English dancer Maud Allan to write a ballet on an Egyptian theme. Besides being a dancer, Maud Allan was apparently a gifted musician who had been a pupil of Busoni, and she had studied painting and sculpture in Italy. She was certainly no mere cabaret dancer, as has been suggested – though Debussy seems to have had little respect for her, referring to her rather contemptuously in correspondence with his publisher as 'la girl anglaise'. In devising the scenario of the *légende dansée, Khamma,* Maud Allan collaborated with W. L. Courtney, who was a lecturer in philosophy at Oxford, a literary and dramatic critic, and one-time literary editor of the London *Daily Telegraph.* Together they devised this example of a form of choreographic art which combined music, drama and the visual arts.

At the time Debussy was a sick man and in financial difficulties. He accepted the commission – though he seems to have rather disliked the idea, as he disliked any project that he accepted mainly for material reasons. The result is a curious work, lasting about twenty minutes, which bears the stamp of Debussy's style, but which fails to come to life musically – as though he were never really with it in spirit. The fragmentary, elusive music consists largely of effects, rather than extended composition – closely reflecting the stage action, as we find in *Jeux,* but without any of the musical meaning, purpose and inner continuity of *Jeux.*

The scene is the temple of the Egyptian sun-god Amun-Ra. The quiet but ominous opening music, with distant trumpet calls, suggests the plight of a city which is besieged and in grave danger. The High Priest implores the god to deliver the people from their enemies; but there are no favourable signs. The music reflects the supplication, the uncertainty and the terror. Khamma, the dancing girl, is brought into the temple. Musically, the atmosphere changes. Eventually she begins a series of dances of propitiation, which give the composer immense scope for contrast and variety – beginning with the portrayal of fear, and gradually gaining confidence; then becoming ecstatic, reaching a triumphant climax in which the god is appeased and the city is saved. In a crash of thunder Khamma falls to the ground, dead. She has been sacrificed for her people. Distant trumpet-calls this time portray victory, and the rejoicing crowd gradually approaches the temple. The doors are thrown open and the High Priest and his throng enter. The joyous orchestral sounds are quickly stifled as the crowd catches sight of Khamma's dead body, and the ballet ends with the

High Priest giving her his blessing. All is now calm, but a final distant fanfare is a reminder of the ever-present fear of forces beyond human control.

Debussy completed a piano score, but orchestrated very little of it. The composer Charles Koechlin was entrusted with the orchestration, under Debussy's supervision. In the end Debussy liked the work sufficiently to write a revised version and to want to dedicate it to Madame Jacques Durand, the wife of his publisher. And in a letter he referred to 'this curious ballet', with its distant trumpet fanfares 'which send a shiver down your back'.

LA BOÎTE À JOUJOUX

Debussy, like Ravel, was strongly attracted to the unspoilt and uncomplicated world of childhood, with its particular directness and with its own world of imagination and fantasy. In 1913, five years before his death, he wrote the children's ballet *La Boîte à ioujoux* ('The Toy-Box') to a scenario suggested by André Hellé, an illustrator of children's books. 'Toy-boxes', Hellé has explained, 'are really towns in which toys live like real people. Or perhaps towns are nothing else but boxes in which people live like toys.' Debussy found this idea especially congenial; he completed a sketch of the music, but orchestrated only the first few bars. Then the project was set on one side, as there was no hope of performance during the war. After the composer's death, André Caplet completed the orchestration: he had been Debussy's friend and amanuensis for a number of years and knew his style as well as Eric Fenby knew Delius's. The first performance as a ballet was given in Paris at the Théâtre Lyrique de Vaudeville in 1919.

Musically, the work cannot be regarded as important. It has not the sustained musical invention of Debussy's piano suite *The Children's Corner*, though with the interest focused also on the stage action it could undoubtedly be an attractive entertainment for children and grown-ups alike. It certainly made a favourable impression when first performed. The *Monde Musical* wrote: 'What charming music! It is of our own day with its novel rhythms and musical patterns, yet it belongs to all time . . .' The composer was very modest about the aims of the work: he described it as 'panto-mime', and as 'the kind of music I have written for children in Christmas and New Year albums . . . something to amuse the children – nothing more!' It was intended in the first place for his little daughter Chou-Chou. Debussy said that he had taken pains to gain the confidence of the toys belonging to his daughter, in order to capture the correct toy-box atmosphere. And so we have a work lasting about half-an-hour and consisting of a prelude, three scenes and an epilogue, scored for an orchestra which includes celeste, harp and piano, and with percussion instruments much in evidence. The subject is a drama of jealousy and intrigue among the inmates of a toy-box. We have musical-box effects, parody, humour, snatches of folk-song (including *Il était une bergère*) satirically presented, an ingenious *Leitmotiv* technique applied to the different personages, and various kinds of dances, marches and cake-walks. A wooden soldier (English) dances to music closely resembling the famous *Golliwogg's Cake-Walk*. There are brief reminiscences of opera – including the Soldiers' Chorus from *Faust* – and of Mendelssohn's *Wedding March*. Debussy told his publisher, Jacques Durand: 'I have tried to be clear and even amusing, without any kind of pose'.

FANTAISIE FOR PIANO AND ORCHESTRA (1889–90)
The strange thing about the early *Fantaisie* is that it was engraved in 1890, and Debussy was sent a proof; he admired the engraver's work, but never agreed to it being published. A performance was to have taken place in 1890 at a concert of the Société Nationale, conducted by Vincent d'Indy. But at the rehearsal stage Debussy withdrew it and would never as long as he lived allow it to be played. (At that same concert, incidentally, the song *Dansons la Gigue* by Charles Bordes – to the tune of 'The Keel Row', which Debussy used in *Gigues* – was performed. That is where Debussy may well have first encountered the tune.) Not till thirty years later, and after the composer's death, was the *Fantaisie* performed and published.

The work is firmly based in clear tonality throughout (despite some whole-tone touches). The orchestration is carefully worked out, but Debussy (according to Robert Godet) considered it too heavy. Also the particular kind of 'theme and variations' structure used was one which he disliked. There is elegance and youthful exuberance, but Debussy's real character does not clearly emerge. Instead, we feel the spirit of *le père séraphique,* César Franck, and his *Variations Symphoniques* hovering over the work. The chromaticism of the slow movement is cloying and hardly characteristic, even at that stage; and the final movement, though pleasant enough, has a somewhat mechanical feel about its construction.

SOME ARRANGEMENTS

Ravel, as an act of homage after the composer's death, orchestrated two early pieces by Debussy. One was the *Sarabande*, antique in flavour (owing much to the spirit of Erik Satie) – the slow movement of the suite *Pour le Piano*. The other was a light and attractive piece called *Tarantelle styrienne,* dating from 1890. Ravel renamed the latter simply *Danse* in its orchestral form, when it appeared in 1923.

Another pleasant trifle is Debussy's waltz for piano *La Plus que lente*, of 1910, which he later orchestrated himself – 'for the countless *five o'clock* tea-parties frequented by beautiful listeners whom I remembered'. An exotic flavour was added by the use of the gipsy cimbalom (now familiar to concert-goers through its use in the suite from Kodály's *Háry János*).

BERCEUSE HÉROÏQUE

Sadly, the last orchestral work of Debussy was the 'patriotic' war piece of 1914, *Berceuse héroïque*, which he did not want to write. This came about when the novelist Hall Caine approached leading figures in the arts of the allied countries for tributes to the King of the Belgians. *King Albert's Book* was published by the London *Daily Telegraph*; and besides Debussy, contributors included Elgar, Edward German and Massenet. 'Approached by *The Daily Telegraph*,' Debussy said afterwards, 'I was obliged to write something for *King Albert's Book*.' The piece bears the inscription: 'pour rendre hommage à sa Majesté le Roi Albert Premier de Belgique et ses soldats'. Effective use is made of the Belgian national anthem, *La Brabançonne,* treated in typical Debussyan style. Debussy completed a piano version of this four-minute work, then orchestrated it late in 1914 (for a full symphony orchestra, including two harps). The first performance was conducted by his friend Camille Chevillard the following year. Except for *Jeux*, Debussy was not at his best when writing to order. The *Berceuse héroïque*, though not one of his inspired and memorable pieces, fulfils its purpose seriously and adequately. But the real Debussy made music only to serve his art: he wanted to express in music only what he really felt.